CHINA AFTER MAO

China after Mao

BY A. DOAK BARNETT

With Selected Documents

PRINCETON UNIVERSITY PRESS

PRINCETON, NEW JERSEY

1967

Printed in the United States of America
by Princeton University Press, Princeton, New Jersey

To

Katherine Hathaway Barnett

In the hope that some day she may know China

ACKNOWLEDGMENTS

I would like to express my appreciation to Donald W. Klein for reading and commenting on the manuscript, Kenneth Lieberthal for certain research assistance in checking the manuscript, Mary Schoch for preparing the manuscript for publication, and Marjorie Putney for copyediting.

CONTENTS

CONTENTS

PART I

CHAPTER I

Unresolved Problems and Dilemmas

COMMUNIST CHINA has entered a transitional period of great historic significance. The end of the long period of Mao Tse-tung's personal leadership of the Chinese revolution is in sight, and the struggle for succession has begun. Even more important, the entire take-over generation of Chinese revolutionary leaders will soon pass from the scene. These men, who have clung to power and aged in office ever since 1949, realize that before long they will be succeeded by new men, whom Mao has called the "heirs of the revolution," with consequences for the regime that cannot be clearly foreseen but will obviously be profound.

Finally, and perhaps most important, the entire revolution in China has entered an uncertain stage. Despite impressive accomplishments, the regime is still far from achieving many of its basic goals, and it faces unsolved problems and dilemmas of great magnitude. Its aging leaders have been engaged for some time in a process of intense soul-searching, groping for effective strategies to ensure the continuation of uninterrupted revolution at home and abroad.

Over time, groups with varying outlooks, perspectives, and priorities have steadily emerged in China, and in every important field of policy—ideological, political, economic, and military—significant differences of opinion have become evident. Policy debates have concerned a wide range of specific issues, but underlying them all are some basic questions about the future of the revolution in China. Top Chinese Communist leaders now cannot avoid asking themselves: Can the present character of the revolution be preserved, and its momentum sustained, on the basis of Maoist traditions and prescriptions for the future? Or will the forces of "revisionism" transform or even undermine the revolution? Non-Communist observers are asking similar questions, but most would phrase them somewhat differently. Are intractable social problems and human characteristics, the inner logic of the revolutionary process itself, and the passage of time plus the process of modernization, destined to transform the character of the revolution in China? If so, how? In short, will changing conditions make Maoism obsolete?

Clearly, China is approaching the end of an era, and a new stage in the Chinese revolution lies immediately ahead. The country has entered a period in which there will be a greater fluidity of both leadership and policies than at any time since the Communists' take over of power. No one, inside China or out, can really predict with any accuracy what will emerge from this transitional period. But it is important to try, on the basis of the information available, to analyze the major problems which the regime faces, the forces now at work, and the possible directions of future change, because the outcome of developments in China will obviously be of tremendous importance, not only to the fifth of mankind that lives within Peking's domain, but to the rest of the world as well.

The current upheaval in China—symbolized by the so-called great proletarian cultural revolution and the mobilization of China's youth into the Red Guards—are important manifestations of the processes of change now under way. However, in this brief discussion I would like to focus primarily not on the latest headlines but on forces and trends that help to explain them. I will start by analyzing some of the basic unsolved problems and dilemmas that face Peking's leaders, then consider Mao's prescriptions for how to carry on the revolution at home and abroad, and finally discuss possible future changes in Chinese Communist leadership and the consequences they may have for China's policies.

The course of political development in a revolutionary and modernizing society such as that in China is inevitably determined not only by the ability of the revolutionary regime to maintain an effective apparatus of political control, but also by its effectiveness over time in coping successfully with the major problems which face the society it rules, in sustaining some sense of progress and momentum in its programs for change, and in fulfilling at least some of the aspirations aroused by its promises. The revolution makes it difficult for either the rulers or the ruled simply to accept a new status quo, even if the level of achievement is higher than that which prevailed in the old order out of which the revolution emerged. The forces of change released by social revolution and economic and political modernization create a dynamic situation, in which the population—and most specifically the new ruling elite itself—put forward demands that cannot be satisfied if there is a sense of actual or impending stagnation. In short, the standard for success is continued dynamism and sustained progress toward the society's goals.

It is difficult, however, for such a regime to fulfill its many promises, maintain the degree of dynamism characteristic of the initial period of revolutionary rule, and cope successfully with changing problems and demands. Many of the inherited and enduring problems of society are extremely refractory, and progress toward solving them is likely, at best, to be harder and slower than was originally hoped. The "habits of the old society"—a term the Chinese Communists often use—may be successfully repressed in the initial period of the revolution, but over time they have a tendency to reemerge, and old values, ways of thought, and patterns of behavior challenge or erode many of those introduced by the revolution.

The revolutionary leaders, themselves, as they age, are likely to become less adaptable—even if they persist in their revolutionary ardor and commitment—and the temptation is strong to apply old solutions to new problems. They are also, as rulers, likely to be more remote from the real problems of society than they were as grass-roots leaders of a mass revolutionary movement. Moreover, as time passes and society evolves, new groups—and new leaders—inevitably appear, with values and goals that differ from those of the take-over generation of revolutionaries. For all of these reasons the demands on the regime change.

These factors work over time for change in many of the policies evolved in the initial stage of the revolution and even in the nature of the political system itself. The question is really not whether there will be change but rather when, and what the scope and nature of the changes will be.

If one analyzes the 17-year period since the Communist regime was established in China, it seems clear that although in the first decade of its existence, throughout the 1950's, the regime's accomplishments were impressive and a remarkable sense of revolutionary momentum was maintained, since about 1960 the momentum of revolution has declined and its future course of development has been uncertain.

Mao and his closest colleagues have strongly resisted pressures for change in the regime's basic character, or fundamental policies, and have tried to preserve time-tested methods of dealing with the problems they face. But in recent years they have not been able, as in earlier days, to define a clear strategy of action that promises to accelerate, or even to sustain, China's march toward achievement of their major goals.

It would be a great error, however, to underestimate the accomplishments of the Chinese Communists under Mao's leadership, and no analysis of the problems they face, now and in the future, should overlook them.

In their struggle for power, especially after Mao achieved undisputed leadership of the Party in 1935, they created a disciplined revolutionary movement unprecedented in Chinese history, evolved a distinctive revolutionary strategy that successfully appealed to nationalism as well as to the forces of peasant revolt in China, and won their struggle for power against odds which at first seemed insuperable.

After establishing a new regime in 1949, they rapidly consolidated their political power and embarked upon very ambitious programs of social change and economic development which have clearly made an indelible imprint on Chinese society. Under Mao's tutelage, the leadership until recently, at least, has maintained a unity that seems almost unique in the history of revolutionary regimes. They have built the largest mass party in history, and have kept it under tight discipline. They have unified mainland China, nurtured a new ruling elite at every level of society, indoctrinated the population in a new official ideology, and restructured all class relationships.

With their monopoly of political power, and an effective apparatus of totalitarian organization that extends central power to the lowest levels of society as never before, they have changed the face of China in fundamental ways. They have socialized and collectivized the economy and initiated a significant program of industrialization. The basis of modern military power has been built, and for the first time in the modern period, China's influence has been projected far beyond its borders.

In short, within just a few years of achieving power —in fact, within the first decade—the Chinese Communists were able to reintegrate a disintegrating society, stimulate a process of growth in an economy that had been stagnating, and revolutionize the social structure of one of the world's most ancient societies. They were also able to create the foundations of modern industrial and military power to fill what had long been a power vacuum, and they soon transformed a nation that for decades had been a pawn in international affairs into an important power with growing influence on the world stage.

In looking to the future, however, the past accomplishments of the regime may not be as relevant for an understanding of the possible course of future events as the unresolved problems and dilemmas still confronting Communist China's leaders and the difficult policy choices which they face. Many of Peking's most basic dilemmas relate to the central question of how to promote sustained economic development and growth.

Unresolved Problems and Dilemmas

When the Communists first came to power, their primary economic task was simply that of rehabilitating the economy which they had inherited, although they were determined at the same time to initiate a process of social revolution designed to break down the fabric of the old society and lay the groundwork for future collectivization and socialization. The "period of rehabilitation," as they called it, lasted for roughly three years, from 1949 through 1952, and was notably successful. Moving into the vacuum created by the collapse of the old order, they applied mobilizational skills and techniques perfected during their struggle for power and, despite their lack of knowledge concerning many of the problems of modern development, they were able in short order to get China's farms and industries producing again. Mao's theory of "new democracy," which called for temporary toleration and utilization of cooperative capitalists, served them well in this period, and the restoration of unity and order was in itself a major factor speeding rehabilitation. By late 1952, despite the Korean War, the Chinese economy was producing at levels close to its prewar peaks, and Peking's leaders were ready to move to a new stage in their revolution.

In 1953 the Chinese Communists initiated their first Five Year Plan. "Socialization" and "industrialization" now became the regime's key slogans, and Peking embarked on an ambitious program of development, with the Soviet Union as its model. Even though no long-term plan was really adopted until mid-1955—after Stalin had died, the Korean truce had been signed, and the Russians had indicated what assistance they would provide—nevertheless the first Five Year Plan did, in a very real sense, usher in an important new stage of development.

The Plan, and Peking's "General Line of the State for the Period of Transition to Socialism," which was also defined in 1953, were clearly modeled on previous experience in the Soviet Union. They called for overall state planning, collectivization of agriculture, socialization of industry and commerce, a high level of investment in industry, tight controls on consumption, and a rapid overall rate of growth. The Chinese Communists self-consciously emulated Soviet techniques of planning and management, and although they adapted much of what they borrowed, and persisted in using many of their own distinctive "mass-line" methods of social mobilization, the first Five Year Plan followed paths already pioneered by the Russians.

On balance, this second period, like the first, was impressively successful. Collectivization and socialization were carried out with a minimum of disruption; and in this period Communist China was able to achieve a growth rate—variously estimated as 6 to 8 per cent per year, in terms of GNP—that put it in the forefront of the major developing nations. New industries and industrial centers began to sprout throughout China. Overall industrial output more than doubled. And the production of key heavy industries—such as steel, pig iron, coal, electric power, cement, and machine building—doubled, tripled, or even quadrupled.

However, despite this success, by 1957, the final year of the Plan period, China's rate of growth began to slacken, and many fundamental problems started to "catch up" with the regime. Agricultural output lagged seriously, barely keeping ahead of population growth, and this not only resulted in critical food shortages but also contributed to a general slowdown of growth. Moreover, there seemed to be no immediate prospect for rapid agricultural improvement; collectivization had not resulted in any dramatic rise in output and, in fact, contributed to short-term difficulties.

Managerial problems of many sorts, in both industry and agriculture, plagued the regime. Planning errors, which had resulted in overexpansion, necessitated a sharp cutback in plans; this involved the first reduction in the state budget since the Plan had begun, a slash in the capital construction budget, and a significant slowdown in industrial expansion. The ending of Soviet credits to China, and the necessity of paying back past credits, created additional strains by making it more difficult for Peking to import the capital goods needed to push forward a program of industrialization of the sort promoted during the first Plan period.

These economic factors argued, therefore, for some new approach to national development, a different

strategy that could halt the decline and stimulate renewed progress toward the regime's goals.

Economic factors were reinforced by the political
crisis which China experienced in the same period.
Starting in 1956, the regime began to loosen its controls and improve its treatment of China's intellectuals
and technicians, hoping to maximize their contribution
to the nation's development programs. The Polish and
Hungarian crises, following Khrushchev's "de-Stalin-
ization," stimulated Mao to reexamine China's own
internal tensions and problems. As a result, Peking
first launched a new "rectification" campaign within
the Communist Party, to tighten discipline among the
faithful. Subsequently, in May-June 1957, it lifted the
lid on free expression of opinion and launched a full-
scale campaign to encourage open criticism by intellectuals and others.

The resulting flood of criticism, during this "100
flowers" period, revealed widespread dissidence. The
attacks, which went far beyond what the Party considered to be legitimate criticism and challenged some
of the fundamental principles and assumptions on
which Communist rule was based, came as a traumatic
shock to Peking's leaders. As is well known, the Party
tolerated the attacks for only a brief period and then
quickly tightened political controls again, embarked
on a tough "anti-Rightist" campaign, and stepped up
its efforts to indoctrinate the entire population. The
net result was a new sense of urgency among Peking's

leaders about the need for dramatic steps to revitalize the revolution.

Some time in the fall of 1957—possibly at the Central Committee plenum in September-October—the leadership decided on a radical new approach. It had been moving slowly in new directions since the Eighth Party Congress in late 1956, and steps toward economic decentralization, increased attention to agriculture, and greater stress on self-reliance hinted at things to come. But the new approach adopted in late 1957 soon led to dramatic, unprecedentedly radical steps—even for China—toward mass mobilization and accelerated institutional change. The regime's program unfolded, with gathering momentum, throughout late 1957 and 1958—first with a huge effort to mobilize tens of millions of peasants for work on water conservancy projects, then proclamation of the Great Leap Forward and a new "General Line of the State for the Construction of Socialism," which involved total mobilization of the country's population for frantic efforts to expand output in both agriculture and industry, and finally the establishments of the Communes.

It is difficult to summarize the remarkable developments of the Great Leap period in a few words. The entire working force was mobilized to try to accomplish the impossible by sheer will and work. Ideological exhortation replaced material incentives. An attempt was made to substitute labor for capital wherever possible. Untested technical innovations such as deep plowing and close planting, in the field of agriculture, and the "backyard steel furnaces," in the field of industry, were promoted throughout the nation. Armies of peasant workers were assigned to nurture each plant in the fields and to build thousands of small-scale rural industries.

At the same time, the regime tried, as it put it, to "walk on two legs" and to speed up the growth of modern large-scale industry as well as smaller enterprises. The labor force was militarized, and militia forces were established everywhere, to make "everyone a soldier." Birth control measures, which had been initiated, however haltingly, in the previous period, were now abandoned, and Peking proclaimed that China's huge population was its major asset, not a problem. Peking's leaders claimed, in fact, that China had a labor shortage, and for a brief period this may in a sense have been the case.

Central planning was, for all practical purposes, abandoned, and extreme economic decentralization was carried out. Policy impulses and ideological exhortation continued to emanate from Peking, and control over the population at a grass-roots level was tightened, but is was the local cadres who were responsible for producing results, by whatever methods they could devise.

The Communes, huge multipurpose units each containing an average of about 5,000 families, combined local government with the collectives. They were exhorted to push local development on the basis of their own resources. In some respects they appeared to be a logical new institutional device to carry out the Great-Leap program, since some institutional innovation was obviously required to handle the many new tasks demanded of the population.

In essence the Great Leap and Communes represented an attempt to "get over the hump" in solving China's basic problems of development in one heroic effort. They were based on Mao's utopian faith that a proper combination of ideological incentives, human will, and effective organization can overcome any problem and achieve any goal. They constituted, as some have put it, a guerrilla warfare approach to development. The regime rejected the arguments of those who maintained that modernization requires an emphasis on scientific and technical expertise, rational management, economic incentives, and gradualism. It attempted to revitalize ideas and assumptions about how best to manage society and solve human problems which had been evolved, and had worked, during the Chinese Communists' struggle for power.

The most important thing about the Great Leap, viewed from the perspective of today, is that it failed. It is true that for one year, in 1958, as a result of an exceptionally good harvest, agricultural output was raised to a new peak. It is also true that rapid development of large-scale modern industry continued into 1960, partly as a result of the momentum that had developed during the First-Plan period. By late 1960

Peking claimed a steel output of 18 million tons, and while this was probably an exaggeration, impressive growth in the modern industrial sector apparently did take place.

But, starting in 1959, the agricultural sector of the economy encountered disastrous setbacks, and soon the Chinese economy as a whole went into a period of acute depression, which reached its nadir in 1961. The result was worse than economic stagnation; for a while there was very real retrogression.

The reasons for the failure were numerous. Three years of natural disasters were one important factor. So too was the cut off of all Soviet technical assistance to Communist China in 1960, as a result of the mounting Sino-Soviet dispute. But more basic was the fact that the Great-Leap policies themselves were ill-conceived and divorced from reality.

The regime's policies ignored the most basic human demands of the population, and failed to provide even the minimum incentives required for sustained effort. In addition, there was a general managerial breakdown; the lack of rational planning and the Leap's particular forms of decentralization resulted in near-chaos. Many of the untested innovations backfired and resulted in disastrous waste. And the new institutional experiments, most notably the Communes, simply did not work as planned.

Since 1962, the Chinese economy has been recovering slowly from its low point in the immediate post-Leap period, and the period of acute economic crisis has passed. But the process of recovery is not yet complete, and the failures of the Leap have had certain lasting effects which the regime cannot overlook. Moreover, Peking has yet to find any dramatic new formulas to solve China's basic economic dilemmas or to ensure growth, and its leaders are obviously still groping for the best policies to pursue in the future.

Recovery from the worst years of crisis was made possible by a virtual abandonment of both the Leap concept and the Communes. Gradually, the regime made some fairly reasonable adjustments of policy, based on ad hoc improvisation, and tried to take account of reality in order to cope with the country's most pressing problems. Modifications in the Communes started as early as the winter of 1958, and by 1961, while in a formal sense the Communes continued to exist, their basic subunits, the Production Teams, were operating much as the previous collectives had. This, plus the restoration of peasants' "free plots" and the reopening of rural free markets, restored at least a minimum of incentives for the peasant population. All unnecessary work projects were halted. And large-scale food imports were begun.

Starting in 1961, the regime for the first time clearly and unequivocally gave priority to agricultural improvement over industrial development. At roughly the same time it reinstituted a birth control program. Foreign trade was reoriented from the Communist bloc to Japan and Western countries, which were best able to provide both essential food grains and certain crucial industrial plants, such as fertilizer factories, important to agricultural improvement.

In general, industry was allowed to mark time, except in a few critical fields. Apart from military and defense plants, the petroleum industry, and a few other special fields, which continued to receive top priority, the new industrial plants constructed now were mainly those whose products would help spur agricultural development.

As a result of these generally sensible and realistic moves, a degree of economic stability was achieved, and a process of growth renewed, albeit at a very modest rate. But—and this is the key point to note in examining Peking's present policy dilemmas—no clear course of action now points toward new and dependable means to accelerate growth, and this fact is clearly a source of great frustration for Communist China's impatient revolutionary leaders.

Total agricultural output even today is believed to be at approximately the same level, in absolute terms, as it was in 1957, before the Great Leap, and in per capita terms, therefore, it is still considerably below that level. Despite growth in a few key fields, total industrial production today is believed to be well below its previous peak, and there is still unused capacity lying idle in some industries. (I use the term "believed to be," because Peking has not published any general economic statistics since 1960.)

Moreover, there is reason to believe that Communist China has not really had any effective, overall, long-term, national economic plan in operation for over eight years—for almost half the time it has been in existence. The second plan was abandoned at its start, in favor of the Great Leap. It was not until this year that a third plan was even formally instituted, and there is still good reason to be skeptical as to whether it is, as yet, a fully operative long-term plan.

In a deep and fundamental fashion, also, in the post-Leap period the regime lost much of the élan that characterized its early years. After the traumatic failures of the Leap, the leaders themselves became more uncertain about the correct course of future action, and less optimistic about the possibility of achieving their goals rapidly. The population at large became more cynical about promises of millennial achievements, more skeptical about claims concerning the infallibility of China's leadership, and less susceptible to massive Party-directed mobilizational efforts.

The uneasiness of the top leadership about the dangers of stagnation, and the possibility of degeneration of the revolution, grew during this period and soon led to steps in the ideological and political fields designed to create a renewed sense of revolutionary momentum. As early as the fall of 1962, in fact, when the first signs of a significant upturn in the economy became evident, the Party Central Committee at its Tenth Plenum acted to call a halt to what it felt to be a serious deterioration of revolutionary morale. Ever since then China has moved steadily in the direction of increased political radicalization.

The leaders first mounted new, massive "socialist education" and Party "rectification" campaigns. They put renewed emphasis on the deification of Mao and all his works. They fostered village-level class struggle once again, renewed the campaign to organize local militia throughout the nation, transferred huge numbers of people from the cities to the countryside, established political commissars in the economic agencies of the government to tighten controls, renewed attacks on China's intellectuals, abolished all symbols of rank in the Chinese army—and in general attempted to combat "bourgeois" and "revisionist" influences, promote revolutionary values, and create a sense of dynamic tension and forward motion. The current cultural revolution and Red Guard campaign are the latest manifestations of this effort to "revolutionize" Chinese society once again.

But to a remarkable degree, Peking's domestic economic policies—and the leaders responsible for them—appear to have been little affected to date by these political moves. In the past, radicalization has tended to take place simultaneously in both political and economic fields, but now there appears to be a mixture of seemingly contradictory, and in some respects incompatible, economic and political policies. So far, at least, a relatively pragmatic approach to economic policy, calling for ad hoc solutions to concrete problems, continues, despite the "revolutionizing" of politics.

There are reasons to believe that the present mixture of policies reflects a compromise between the conflicting forces at work within the regime. These forces are increasingly complex, but in oversimplified terms one can differentiate between two poles in a spectrum of opinion, and these appear to be exerting pressures in very different directions.

On the one side are those who still have great faith in the effectiveness of ideological and political mobilization of the sort that served the Party well in earlier years. Mao himself clearly persists in this faith, as do many other top leaders. On the other side, however, there now appear to be persons at all levels in the regime who, after struggling for years with the practical problems of administration and development, incline toward a more pragmatic, less dogmatic, and less ideological approach to problems. These men, who are undoubtedly most strongly represented among China's economic administrators, technical-bureaucrats, and specialists of all sorts, are the ones who tend to be skeptical of visionary "upsurges" and seemingly favor relatively pragmatic, realistic, and moderate policies.

Men in the first category insist that it is essential to maintain a high state of tension and ideological fervor in China in order to sustain revolutionary momentum and ensure a rapid pace of change. They fear that otherwise, over time, the revolution will be gravely weakened by erosion and might fundamentally change its character.

Those in the second category seem prepared—in relative terms at least—to acknowledge that the present problems of modernization and development differ from the earlier problems of revolutionary struggle. They apparently recognize that effective management, scientific and technical skills, and economic incentives are required for success in economic development and modernization, and that organizational mobilization and ideological indoctrination are not enough to do the job. At least some of them seem prepared to recognize that change will, of necessity, have to take place at a more gradual rate than was possible in earlier years.

To date, in the interplay of forces that has taken place in China in recent years, while Mao and other militant Maoists have successfully insisted on pushing toward increasing radicalization of the regime's political line, the pragmatists—who doubtless include some of China's leading administrators and technical-bureaucrats—have apparently been successful in demanding that economic policies must take account of economic realities. So far, at least, they seem to have insisted successfully that at least minimum economic incentives must be provided to the people, and that visionary big pushes are not feasible under existing conditions—even though this probably does mean acceptance of a fairly moderate rate of economic growth for the immediate future.

However, in many respects the current mixture of policies is not a stable one. It remains to be seen, therefore, whether the mixture will be preserved, or whether the anomalies will be resolved in the future, either by a move toward greater pragmatism and moderation in *both* politics and economics, or by a move toward greater dogmatism and radicalism in *both*.

Which way China moves is obviously one of the crucial questions for the future, and it will pose some of the most difficult policy choices for Mao's successors. Should Communist China intensify its efforts at political and ideological mobilization and then, despite all difficulties, gird itself for more attempted leaps forward in development? Or should the regime come to terms with the enormous problems and difficulties it faces, and adjust to changing social conditions and attitudes at home as well as the changing international environment affecting China?

Should it conclude that development in the future must be more pragmatic and gradual than in earlier years, and on this basis formulate long-term policies which stress steady agricultural growth, population control, and industrialization of a balanced sort at a realistic rate? Should it accept the proposition that for such policies to be successful, less stress should be placed on political controls and ideological indoctrination, and more on scientific and technical competence and increased material incentives for the population? And should it, if it pursues such policies at home, change its posture abroad, adopting less militant policies, which would reduce the strain on China's scarce resources and help build relationships with other nations that indirectly or directly might provide support for the nation's domestic development programs?

The dilemmas and policy choices facing Peking's leaders in the economic field are really only one facet of an even more fundamental question that relates to virtually every aspect of society and is crucial to the future course of developments in China. The Chinese Communists, with their genius for coining slogans, have summed this up as the "red and expert" problem. The regime's aim has been to create a new generation that would be both "red and expert" or, to translate this slogan into more familiar terms, both ideologically motivated, loyal servants of the revolution and technically proficient specialists capable of performing the varied and complex tasks required in a modernizing society. While both "redness" and "expertness" are recognized to be important, however, Mao and the leaders who are now dominant clearly insist on "redness" above all, and if faced with a choice, they would prefer "reds" who are not "expert" to "experts" who are not "red." They have a deep, and well-justified, apprehension that specialization and technical expertise may tend to undermine the kind of commitment to ideological dogma that they believe to be necessary to continue the sort of revolution which they think China must undergo.

In reality, there has been a growing dichotomy between "reds" and "experts" throughout the society in China, and the differences between them can be expected to continue and increase in the future. Not only has this dichotomy created significant tensions in the relations between the men running the Party apparatus and key groups in the country—including, for example, professional military leaders, intellectuals, and economic managers—but there is evidence that over time there have been trends toward increasing functional specialization and differentiation within the Party apparatus itself, and these trends have almost certainly affected the outlooks and policy preferences of different groups of top Party members in differing ways.

Mao's idealized conception of the sort of man required to keep up the revolutionary struggle is one who is wholly obedient to Party discipline, loyal and dedicated to the regime's goals, self-sacrificing and unconcerned about his personal welfare, and always willing to place the good of the revolution as a whole —as defined by the Party's leaders—above parochial interests or specialized concerns. The irony of the situation, however, is that the process of modernization requires, and helps to create, specialists who tend to value professional competence over ideological commitment and who are likely to push for at least some policies of a kind that the present top leaders in China call "revisionist." In short, the consequences of modernization are likely to erode the basis of continuing revolutionary dogmatism and ardor—at least by the standards still maintained by Mao and his closest colleagues.

Another related problem has been the growing trend toward bureaucratization and routinization in China, in the Party as well as in the government, which also is seen by the leaders who are now dominant in Peking as threatening to undermine the revolutionary character of the regime. Despite all the top leaders' efforts, old bureaucratic patterns of behavior have reemerged, and the Party and government cadres in China have increasingly become an elite set apart from the population. This elite, moreover, is highly stratified and rank-conscious. To a remarkable degree, however, the present Chinese Communist leaders have persisted in their efforts to promote what they call a "mass-line style of politics," and to implement their major policies through "mass campaigns" or crash programs. But for many reasons it has become increasingly difficult for the regime to achieve many of its goals by such methods.

The population is clearly weary of Party-promoted mass campaigns, which demand frenetic activity on everyone's part. Furthermore, the increasingly complex and specialized tasks of modernization have demanded

Unreolved problems

Unresolved Problems and Dilemmas

greater regularization, and to some extent routinization, of administration to implement the regime's policies. Mobilizational campaigns, such as the current cultural revolution and Red Guard drive, which are based mainly on mass effort by well-indoctrinated but unskilled manpower, can arouse passions, create tensions, and stir up the country, but they do not raise agricultural productivity, increase industrial output, or solve other basic problems.

I cannot in this brief discussion describe in detail how basic problems and dilemmas of the sort I have mentioned affect groups throughout society, posing unresolved policy dilemmas for Peking's leaders. But to illustrate, let me give just a few examples.

The Chinese Communist military establishment faces a very fundamental "red and expert" problem. It has experienced a steady growth of professionalism, since the mid-1950's, which has led to increasing differences on many issues among military leaders, between officers and members of the Party apparatus who supervise them, and within the military establishment between different generations of officers.

The elements of conflict have been numerous. They have involved differences over the degree to which external controls, through Party committees and political commissars, should be exercised over military units, the extent to which traditional Maoist principles stressing "men over weapons" should be preserved or new nuclear-age concepts should be accepted, the feasibility of preserving equalitarian traditions in relations between officers and men and promoting "mass-line" patterns of relations between the army and civilians, the extent to which military personnel should be used for economic and other nonmilitary tasks, and the value of nonprofessional militia. They have also involved fundamental differences over the implications of China's military situation and needs for the country's foreign policy—most specifically policy toward the Soviet Union.

Some military men have questioned the wisdom of basic domestic policies, including those involved in the Great Leap Forward. In the immediate post-Leap period, morale within the army sagged dangerously. However, following the purging of P'eng Teh-huai as Defense Minister in 1959 and the appointment of Lin Piao as his successor, an intense program of indoctrination was implemented throughout the military forces, Maoist principles were reemphasized (although development of atomic weapons was pushed at the same time), and Party dominance was emphatically reasserted. All of this was done with apparent success, for the army was soon held up as the model of ideological and organizational excellence which the rest of society has been exhorted to emulate, many military leaders have risen to positions of new prominence, and Lin Piao has emerged as Mao's designated heir.

But the regime still feels compelled to devise new measures to combat trends toward professionalism, and clearly the basic dilemmas have not been solved once and for all.

Despite the support given by Lin Piao and other military leaders to the current efforts to revolutionize and politicize society, over the long run the pressures to emphasize professional competence and reduce political controls in the army—that is, to stress "expertness" rather than "redness"—are almost certain to increase rather than decrease. Even if Lin Piao succeeds to Mao's position of top leadership, therefore, he will find it difficult to maintain the army as an ideologically oriented, Party-dominated revolutionary force that operates on Maoist principles, for there will be continuing demands for steps toward increased professionalization and modernization.

The Party has had serious and growing problems in its relations with China's intellectuals. It is not overstating the case, in fact, to say that it has really failed in its efforts to date to "remold" them, as a group, or to work out a mutually acceptable, stable basis for harmonious collaboration over the long run. Since the early 1950's the Party has repeatedly organized campaigns which have subjected the intellectuals to intensive "thought reform." Sizeable numbers of intellectuals have been absorbed into the Party, where they are subject to direct Party discipline. But a very large number of them have insisted on maintaining at least a degree of intellectual independence, refusing to submit totally to Party controls or to accept unquestioningly Party-defined dogma.

As a group, therefore, the intellectuals, too, have resisted the Party's efforts to make "redness" more important than "expertness," and they can be expected to continue doing so in the future. For more than two years, another major indoctrination campaign has been in progress to suppress "revisionist tendencies" in China, and the intellectuals have again been subjected to tightened political controls. But there is very little reason to believe that this campaign will fundamentally "remold" them any more successfully than past efforts of a similar sort.

The problem, it should be noted, has not been confined simply to old intellectuals, inherited from the previous regime. Peking's leaders have shown growing concern about the newly educated younger generation who, as they see it, have lacked the kind of commitment to revolutionary values that the first generation of Party leaders have shared, because they have not known from personal experience the "evils of pre-Communist society" and have not been "tempered by class struggle." The Red Guards' campaign is testimony to Mao's belief that drastic measures are required to shake up the entire country, including the youth, rather than a sign of unquestioning faith in the younger generation's revolutionary commitment.

The regime's problems in relations with its economic managers have also posed major dilemmas that are by no means finally resolved. Here again, the central question really has been how to mix "reds" and "experts," and the regime has vacillated in its policies, as it has tried to work out a viable relationship between the two groups. In more concrete terms, a key question has been what pattern of relations should be established between the professionally and technically oriented managers of economic enterprises and the Party committees exercising political control within such enterprises.

In the early 1950's, following the Soviet model, a system of management was adopted which concentrated primary authority and responsibility in the managers, restricting the role of Party committees to one of general supervision and ideological indoctrination. In the latter 1950's, the dominance of the Party committees was strongly reasserted, and while the managers were left with major responsibilities they were deprived of ultimate authority, since the Party in effect took over direct control of management. After the retreat from the extremist policies of the Great Leap, the authority of the managers was again increased, and economic power in the enterprises was more broadly distributed. But in 1964, when the regime was movng toward a tightening of controls throughout society, new "political departments"—modeled on the commissar system in the army—were established within all enterprises, in order to reassert central Party direction.

It is questionable whether the existing pattern is one

which can ensure both effective management and reliable political control, and it would be surprising if, over the long run, the "experts" do not increasingly demand, in the name of efficiency, greater authority and less direct interference by either Party committees or commissars.

One could mention a great many other problems, foreign as well as domestic, with which Mao's successors will have to wrestle. The main point to recognize is that the passage of time and the process of social change—combined with the disappearance of Mao—are likely to exert increasing pressures for new and more effective measures to cope with China's problems, and there seems little doubt that there will be greater competition between differing policy proposals and more serious consideration of a variety of policy options which the regime might adopt.

Because of his unique position, Mao himself has been able in recent years to make the crucial decisions on strategy and policy, both at home and abroad. He has been able to impose his own views and to carry along the rest of the leadership, the Party, and the country with him. But no individual after Mao is likely to be able to do this in the same fashion.

In a fundamental sense perhaps the basic choice that will confront Mao's successors will be whether to continue pursuing paths already charted, to adhere to Mao's prescribed course of action, and to try to preserve the character of the revolution and the regime unchanged, or to move in new directions, adapting to evolving conditions and needs, and responding primarily to the imperatives of modernization rather than to the requirements of ideological dogma, even if this demands major changes in the patterns of organization and action that have guided the Chinese Communist regime in the past.

Mao himself is obviously determined to do all he can to ensure continuity in the future. The current upheaval in China can be viewed in one sense as a final apocalyptic effort by Mao—or at least by men who share his vision—to ensure that his successors resist the pressures to move the Chinese revolution in new directions.

CHAPTER II

Mao's Prescriptions for the Future

THERE is no doubt that the period now approaching its end in Communist China will be labeled the Maoist era. Mao Tse-tung has been one of those rare charismatic leaders whose personal imprint has been placed on every aspect of the revolutionary movement he has led and the society he has ruled.

One of the dozen men who met in a small room in Shanghai in 1921 to found the Chinese Communist Party, Mao in the late 1920's and 1930's was the chief designer of the Party's successful strategy of revolution. Since 1935 he has been the unchallengeable leader of the Party, and he has guided all important affairs of state since 1949. Whatever positions he has held—in 1959 he turned over chairmanship of the government to Liu Shao-ch'i but continued to hold the Party Chairmanship—he has for most of his career been the Chinese Communists' principal ideologist, political organizer, military leader, and government administrator. His ideas and personality have permeated the society, and his statements on any and every subject have acquired the force of oracular pronouncements.

There is also no doubt that the Maoist era will draw to a close before long. In December 1966, Mao became 73, and despite great publicity about his ability to swim the Yangtze River—he has been in declining health.

35

Mao's Prescriptions for the Future

The international guessing game about the precise time of his approaching demise is not very fruitful; there is no reliable basis for determining exactly when he will pass from the scene. Nevertheless, it is clear that the era Mao has dominated will end in the relatively near future, and that a new era in the history of the Chinese revolution will then begin.

As Mao has aged, he has been increasingly deified, and the cult of his personality has recently been developed to new and extreme—one might even say absurd—heights. No matter how mundane the problem in Communist China today—whether it is one of winning ping-pong matches or selling watermelon seeds—the name of Mao and the wisdom of his thought are invoked. The entire population has been mobilized to study his works, with an intensity that is remarkable even for Communist China. If there were an international best-seller list, there is little doubt that writings by Mao would occupy most of the leading positions.

The entire leadership in Communist China, including Mao himself, has been acutely aware for some time of the approaching transitional period when he will disappear from the scene, and the current turmoil in China—including not only the extreme efforts to deify Mao, the massive program of general indoctrination, the campaign to "train successors," the current cultural revolution, and the Red Guards' campaign, but also the bitter behind-the-scenes power struggles and policy debates now under way—has in a fundamental sense been stimulated by anticipation of, and preparation for, the time when Mao dies.

Mao's own mood has been described by Edgar Snow as that of a person "reflecting on man's rendezvous with death." In a remarkable interview which he granted to Snow on January 9, 1965, Mao seemed to "let his hair down" in an almost unprecedented fashion and ruminated not only about his own approaching demise but also about the long-run future of the Chinese revolution.[1]

Mao's personal preoccupation with mortality was a recurring theme throughout the interview. He recounted how, over the years, so many persons close to him had been killed (including his first wife, both of his brothers, and a son), described the narrow escapes he himself had had, and said "it was odd that death had so far passed him by." His most startling statement, then, was that he was "getting ready to see God very soon," although he immediately added that he himself did not believe in God.

These reflections on his own death are less significant, however, than the uncertainties which Mao articulated very frankly during the interview about the possible shape of things to come and the future of the

[1] Snow's summary of the interview was checked by another person present at the interview, and Snow was granted permission to publish it, but without direct quotation. The portions quoted here are from that summary, in which they appear without quotation marks, in *The New Republic*, February 27, 1965.

revolution in China. His statements to Snow reveal an intense awareness of the approaching end of an era, and an almost poignant mood of soul-searching. His uncertainties are doubtless shared by many of the leaders in China.

One of the hallmarks of Mao's writings, as well as of his actions, had been the stress he has placed upon the positive role that human will can play in history and the ability of dedicated men to overcome all difficulties and mold the course of events. This fact makes particularly striking the assertion he made to Snow, during his ruminations, that "events do not always move in accordance with human will."

After this statement, he proceeded to express his lurking doubts about the character of the younger generation in China as well as his uncertainties about the future of the revolution. "Those in China now under the age of 20," he said, have "never fought a war and never seen an imperialist or known capitalism in power." He was asked, what will these young men and women, bred under easier conditions, do in the future? Mao replied that he "could not know" and "doubted that anyone could be sure." But, he said, there are "two possibilities." "There could be continued development of the revolution toward Communism," or the "youth could negate the revolution, and give a poor performance: make peace with imperialism, bring the remnants of the Chiang K'ai-shek clique back to the mainland, and take a stand beside the small percentage of counterrevolutionaries still in the country." The mass campaigns now convulsing Chinese society are Mao's attempt to prevent the next generation from "giving a poor performance," but they are not likely to resolve all of his doubts.

In the final analysis, Mao stated to Snow, "future events will be decided by future generations. . . . The youth of today and those to come after them" will "assess the work of the revolution in accordance with values of their own." Then, he declared, in the most startling of all his statements: "Man's condition on earth" is "changing with increasing rapidity. A thousand years from now . . . even Marx, Engels and Lenin" will "possibly appear rather ridiculous."

Snow concluded that Mao's mood showed he was "ready to leave the assessment of his political legacy to future generations," and some of the statements quoted above would seem to imply this. But his public actions, and the present policies of the regime, suggest otherwise. In the intense "socialist education campaign," "cultural revolution," Red Guards' campaign, and political purge that have unfolded in China in recent months, dire warnings about the dangers of subversion of the revolution, by forces both at home and abroad, have been combined with adamant insistence that the "Thought of Mao Tse-tung" be enshrined as sacred gospel to guide the future course of the revolution until its final success, several generations hence.

In short, the present top leaders in China are self-consciously deifying Mao, and propagating his prescriptions for the future, to strengthen the regime against the dangers and challenges that they fear will confront it after his death. Whether Mao himself or other leaders in the regime have been primarily responsible for initiating this effort, Mao clearly endorses the effort and feels it is both necessary and desirable. In his interview with Snow, in fact, he not only admitted that a "cult of personality" had developed in China but, contrasting Khrushchev with Stalin, asked "was it possible that Mr. K. fell because he had no cult of personality at all?"

The degree to which Mao's thought has been glorified in China in recent months far exceeds any such efforts in earlier years. It is true that Mao's ideological creativity in adapting Marxism-Leninism to China was acknowledged as early as the 1930's, that by 1945 the term "Thought of Mao Tse-tung" was incorporated into the Party constitution, and that by 1951 the Chinese Communists were claiming that "Mao Tse-tung's theory of the Chinese revolution is a new development of Marxism-Leninism . . . of universal significance for the world Communist movement . . . a new contribution to the treasury of Marxism-Leninism."[2] It is also true that from the late 1950's on, particularly as the Sino-Soviet dispute increased in intensity, the claims

[2] Statement on July 1, 1951, by Lu Ting-yi, head of the Communist Party Central Committee's Propaganda Department. See *Current Background* (American Consulate-General, Hong Kong), No. 89, July 5, 1951.

regarding Mao's ideological stature steadily escalated. But the extravagance of the current effort to reinforce his ideological authority has reached unprecedented heights, and now the Chinese explicitly place Mao in the pantheon of Communist immortals on a par with Marx, Engels, Lenin, and Stalin.

Many recent statements could be cited to illustrate this development, but perhaps one will suffice. In February 1966, following a meeting of the Central-South China Bureau of the Party Central Committee which declared that the "Thought of Mao" is "the apex of contemporary Marxism," the *Hunan Daily* carried an article (a reprint of a *Yangcheng Evening News* editorial) which gave a new capsulated version of the history of the world revolution. It deserves to be quoted at some length.

"To study the Thought of Mao Tse-tung well," it said, "we must understand its role in this great epoch." The article then analyzed the history of the world Communist movement in terms of three major epochs, as follows.

> The period from the birth of Marxism in the forties of the nineteenth century to the nineties marked the first fifty years of the advance of Marxism. It was a historical stage represented by Marx and Engels. . . . The proletariat had emerged as an independent political power in the arena of the history of mankind. . . .

Mao's Prescriptions for the Future

The period from the late nineties of the nineteenth century to the early fifties of the twentieth century marked the second fifty years of the advance of Marxism. During this period capitalism evolved to the final stage—imperialism. . . . The first socialist state was established. . . .

The revolutionary struggle of the people of the world entered a new stage at the end of World War II. The people's revolutionary forces gained tremendous ground. . . . The Chinese people, one-fourth of the world's population, under the leadership of the Chinese Communist Party and Chairman Mao, freed themselves from the shackles of semicolonialism and semifeudalism and took the road toward socialist revolution and socialist construction. . . . The revolutionary storms continue to surge in the oppressed nations of Asia, Africa, and Latin America. . . .

The great banner representing the development of Marxism-Leninism in our time is the Thought of Mao Tse-tung. The Thought of Mao Tse-tung is an overall and systematically developed Marxism during this new and great revolutionary epoch and is the apex of contemporary Marxism. . . .

We have the great task of carrying out China's socialist revolution to the end and rapidly pushing forward China's socialist construction, on the one hand, and the important duty of supporting world revolution, on the other. These are the tasks entrusted to us in our epoch. In order to fulfill these

important tasks, given to us by history, and to become good fighters for Chairman Mao, the most
fundamental thing for us to do is to arm ourselves
with Marxism-Leninism and the Thought of Mao
Tse-tung.[3]

The Chinese Communists still refer to Mao's ideas
as the "Thought of Mao Tse-tung," and have yet to
adopt the term "Maoism"—although conceivably they
might still do so in the future. But the term Maoism
is increasingly used by others. To what extent is this
valid? The degree of originality of Mao's ideological
writings is a hotly contested subject, and there are
some who refute all claims concerning originality by
declaring—with considerable basis—that almost all the
essential ideological components in his thought can be
traced to earlier Marxist-Leninist writings. This misses
the point, however. Despite the fact that he has not
made very significant ideological contributions on the
level of abstract theory, there is no doubt that he has
selected and emphasized certain ideological propositions, combined them in new patterns, reinterpreted
them to fit China's situation, given them a distinctive
Chinese flavor, and produced a new body of writings
in the field of "applied Marxism-Leninism" that can
legitimately be called Maoism.

To give any general outline of the intellectual con-

[3] Changsha Radio, domestic service, February 3, 1966. Minor
grammatical corrections and translation modifications have been
made in the transcript available to the author.

tent of Maoism would require a detailed analysis of the entire corpus of his writings—and most particularly of the four published volumes of his "Selected Works"—which is obviously something that cannot be attempted here. But a few salient characteristics of his thought are important to keep in mind if one is examining his prescriptions for the future.

First of all, Mao in a basic sense sees all social processes in terms of struggle, conflict, and combat. The concept of the law of contradictions—the dialectical struggle between antithetical forces—is one to which he has given special emphasis. There seems little doubt that in this respect he has been greatly influenced by his long experience as a successful leader of guerrilla warfare. His most original writings have been those concerned with military affairs, and his concepts of guerrilla warfare obviously influence his approach to social action of other sorts. He seems to feel not only that progress stops when struggle ends, but that conditions of combat—simulated if necessary—are required to create the type of men, preserve the sort of values, and promote the necessary processes which are essential for continuing revolution. Ever since achieving power, therefore, he has attempted to create contrived conditions of continuing tension and struggle, and he believes this must be continued until the final victory of Communism. Class struggle must go on, he says, throughout the period of socialism.

Despite his emphasis on class struggle, however, Mao

has also stressed a variety of ideas which transcend class. As a dedicated nationalist as well as a revolutionary, he has constantly appealed to Chinese sentiments of patriotism and national pride. He has frequently represented the Chinese Communist Party as the steward of "the people" rather than of the proletariat alone, in a fashion that some have labeled "populist." He has stressed the crucial role of subjective factors in history, the role of individual human will, and has proclaimed that "men are more important than weapons." He purports to believe that whole classes can be transformed by ideological indoctrination. And he puts extraordinary emphasis on the need for each individual to undergo his own revolution, an intellectual and psychic one. He seems convinced that only if the "revolution for men's minds" can be won—if men can be "remolded" to be "true believers" and dedicated revolutionaries—can the success of the revolution be assured. The struggle to achieve this goal seems, in fact, to be more fundamental to him, in many respects, than the possible effects of abstract social forces. He seems to believe, in short, that remaking men is really the crucial task of the revolution—more essential even than institutional change, technical and scientific modernization, or industrialization, although the latter are obviously very important too.

Mao also has placed great stress, in the past at least, on the necessity of "combining theory and practice," of adapting ideology to concrete situations, and of basing policies on accumulated experience. In fact, he claims that, in his view, his essay "On Practice" is more important even than his article "On Contradictions." This pragmatic element in Mao's thought has served the Communists well in China in the past, and the realism and flexibility with which policies were evolved in earlier years were impressive.

There has been mounting evidence in recent years, however, to suggest that while Mao has continued to pay lip service to the concept of "combining theory and practice," he has actually clung tenaciously to old patterns of thought and behavior, in the face of recent experiences which call into question their continuing efficacy. As Chang Kuo-t'ao—another founder of the Chinese Communist Party and a competitor with Mao for top Party leadership in the 1930's—said to me in a conversation in Hong Kong last year, "increasingly Mao seems to have become a revolutionary romantic who has lost touch with the realities of society."

The entire population of China today is engaged in an orgy of study of Maoism, and in a sense all of Mao's works contain his formulas for how to carry on the revolution. However, there are certain documents published by the Chinese Communists that are particularly revealing, I believe, about Mao's present views on the kind of policies China should pursue in the future to ensure uninterrupted revolution. Here I would like to analyze two of them. Neither, actually, bears

Mao's own signature, but both are invaluable summaries of his basic prescriptions for the future.

One is an article entitled, "On Khrushchev's Phoney Communism and Its Historical Lessons for the World."[4] Written jointly by the editorial departments of the *People's Daily* and *Red Flag*, and published on July 14, 1964, this article was the ninth in a series of blistering Chinese attacks on the Soviet Union. With the imprint of the Central Committee's two main official publications, it summarizes the opinions of the regime's leadership, and after describing in vivid language Peking's view on the danger of erosion of the revolution by "revisionism," it outlines a 15-point program—specifically attributed to Mao—defining his prescriptions for the means to ensure successful continuation of the revolution in China. In many respects, this document is the closest thing we have, at present, to a personal testament of Mao's.

The second article I will discuss is the widely publicized one by Marshal Lin Piao, currently China's top military leader and apparently Mao's newly designated heir. Entitled, "Long Live the Victory of People's War," it was issued on September 2, 1965.[5] This work is clearly and explicitly a summing up of Mao's

[4] The full text has been printed in English as a pamphlet, *On Khrushchov's Phoney Communism and Its Historical Lessons for the World*, by the Foreign Language Press, Peking, 1964. (See Document 1, p. 123)

[5] The full text has been printed in English in *Peking Review*, No. 1965-36, September 3, 1965. (See Document 2, p. 196)

thought on China's world role and the future of the world revolution.

The article on "phoney Communism" reveals an almost obsessive preoccupation on the part of Mao and his closest colleagues with the danger that erosive or corrosive forces at home and abroad could result in retrogression, or even the defeat of the revolutionary struggle within China, and it highlights their determination to do everything possible—using time-tested methods that they have employed in the past—to prevent this from happening. It provides striking testimony, as well, to the impact of the Sino-Soviet dispute on domestic affairs in China.

It also reveals that China's leaders are now much less optimistic about the rapid achievement of their ultimate goals than they were just a few years ago. Whereas in 1958, during the Great Leap Forward and Communization period, Chinese Communist leaders implied, and may actually have believed, that China was on the verge of a crucial developmental breakthrough and the achievement of many of the final goals of Communism, they now acknowledge, as stated in this article, that "the complete victory of socialism cannot be brought about in one or two generations; to resolve this question thoroughly requires five or ten generations or even longer." With the acceptance of this kind of timetable, the question of how revolutionary momentum can be sustained, and revolutionary ideals preserved, for such a long period of time becomes, of course, a matter of utmost importance.

A large part of the article, leading up to Mao's 15-point program for China, consists of a withering indictment of revisionist trends in the Soviet Union, as viewed from Peking, but obviously the purpose is not merely to criticize the Russians; it is intended to hold the Soviet Union up as a "negative example" for the entire Communist world movement, and most specifically for China. Khrushchev's revisionism, the article declares, "sounds the alarm for all socialist countries, including China, and for all Communist and Workers Parties, including the Communist Party of China." The authors then ask: "Is our society today thoroughly clean? . . . No it is not," they say. "Classes and class struggle still remain, the activities of the overthrown reactionary classes plotting a comeback still continue, and we still have speculative activities by new and old bourgeois elements and desperate forays by embezzlers, grafters, and degenerates. There are also cases of degeneration in a few primary organizations; what is more, these degenerates do their utmost to find protectors and agents in the higher leading bodies."

In short, it is clear that the article's bitter attack on Soviet revisionism deals with problems and trends which Mao and other Chinese leaders fear may increasingly afflict Chinese society and undermine the revolution after they have gone.

What is the picture painted of the Soviet Union? It

is a vivid portrait of degeneration—by Peking's present standards. There is no praise for the Russians' achievements in modernization—the scientific and technical progress, the industrial growth, the rising standards of living. Instead, there is only disgust and contempt for the social consequences of these developments—the reputed abandonment of class struggle, the bourgeois character of the society, the increased emphasis on economic incentives and material rewards, and the growing differences and gaps between various groups in the society.

Peking accuses Moscow of wrecking the revolution and undermining the "dictatorship of the proletariat" by promoting concepts of "the state of the whole people" and the "party of the entire people." It declares that class struggle has been abandoned in favor of "peaceful coexistence," "peaceful competition," and "peaceful transition." As material incentives and personal betterment have been increasingly stressed, it claims, the result has been "class polarization" and the domination of society by a "privileged bourgeois stratum" composed of "degenerate elements from among the leading cadres of Party and government organizations, enterprises, and farms as well as bourgeois intellectuals." The Soviet Union, the article declares, "has substituted 'material incentives' for the socialist principle, 'from each according to his ability, to each according to his work' . . . [and] is peddling bourgeois ideology, bourgeois liberty, equality, fraternity and humanity . . . and the reactionary ideas of bourgeois individualism, humanism, and pacifism." This "goulash Communism," says the article, is really just a "variant of bourgeois socialism" or, even worse, a new kind of "capitalism."

Proceeding from this diagnosis of Soviet degeneration, the article then goes on to discuss in more generalized terms the problems of sustaining the momentum of revolution. This general discussion deserves particular attention because it obviously represents the Maoist view on the problems facing all "socialist" (that is, Communist-ruled) states—and most particularly China.

"In socialist society," the article declares, "the overthrown bourgeoisie and other reactionary classes remain strong for quite a long time. . . . They conduct open and hidden struggles against the proletariat in every field. . . . Politically . . . they constantly attempt to overthrow the dictatorship of the proletariat. They sneak into the government organs, public organizations, economic departments, and cultural and educational institutions so as to resist and usurp the leadership of the proletariat. Economically, they employ every means to damage socialist ownership by the whole people and socialist collective ownership and to develop the forces of capitalism. In the ideological, cultural and educational fields, they counterpose the bourgeois world outlook to the proletariat world outlook and try to corrupt the proletariat and other working people with bourgeois ideology."

The article goes on to say that the bourgeoisie's "corrupting effects in the political, economic, ideological and cultural and educational fields, the existence of spontaneous capitalist tendencies among urban and rural small producers, and the influence of the remaining bourgeois rights and the force of habit of the old society, all constantly breed political degenerates in the ranks of the working class and Party and government organizations, new bourgeois elements and embezzlers and grafters in State enterprises owned by the whole people and new bourgeois intellectuals in the cultural and educational institutions and intellectual circles. . . . The political degenerates entrenched in the leading organs are particularly dangerous, for they support and shield the bourgeois elements in organs at lower levels. . . . The old and new bourgeois elements, the old and new rich peasants and degenerate elements of all sorts constitute the social basis of revisionism, and they use every possible means to find agents within the Communist Party. The existence of bourgeois influence is the internal source of revisionism and surrender to imperialist pressure is the external source."

In sum, the article declares: "The development of socialist society is a process of uninterrupted revolution. . . . Throughout the stage of socialism the class struggle between the proletariat and the bourgeoisie in the political, economic, ideological and cultural and educational fields cannot be stopped. It is a protracted, repeated, tortuous and complex struggle. Like the waves of the sea it sometimes rises high and sometimes subsides, is now very calm and now very turbulent. It is a struggle that decides the fate of a socialist society."

The dangers of subversion, as described in this article, sound grim. Do Peking's present leaders actually fear an overthrow of their fundamental political and economic system and a "restoration of capitalism" in a literal sense? This is extremely doubtful. What, then, are they really talking about? What are the dangers that actually concern them? Clearly, they are worried by real and fundamental problems that do, indeed, face China and are likely to face Mao's successors. These are essentially the dangers of erosion. They fear that over time the discipline which the leaders have imposed on the Party and on society as a whole will weaken, that there will be pressures to moderate the harshness of political dictatorship, and that private and personal interests will motivate people more than abstract virtue or long-range goals. They fear that the desire for material improvement will supersede the spirit of self-sacrifice now demanded, that old patterns of social stratification and bureaucratism (the "force of habit of the old society") will emerge, and that impulses toward individual enterprise and material betterment ("spontaneous capitalist tendencies") will reassert themselves. They fear that the spirit of compromise, adjustment, and harmonization of diverse interests ("bourgeois influences") will replace dedication to revolutionary combat and class struggle, and that within the Communist Party itself there will be many (the "political degenerates") who will adjust to and even support these trends.

"How," then, the article asks, "can the restoration of capitalism be prevented? On this question, it says, "Mao Tse-tung has formulated a set of theories and policies, after summing up the practical experience of the dictatorship of the proletariat in China and studying the positive and negative experience of other countries, mainly of the Soviet Union." The article then summarizes the "main contents" of these in Mao's 15 points.

What does Mao prescribe? In essence, he says, any and all erosive forces threatening change in the character of the revolution must be opposed and defeated. The essential nature of the revolution as it developed in earlier years must be preserved with unswerving dedication to struggle, self-sacrifice, austerity, ideological reform, and egalitarianism. Faith must be maintained in the "law of contradictions," for it is conflict that "forces things to move and change." Class struggle is essential, therefore, throughout the socialist period. The Party's "dictatorship" over the "reactionary classes" must continue. Party dominance over the army must be preserved. "Counterrevolutionaries must be suppressed wherever found" by the Public Security apparatus. Economic development must be carried on, with "agriculture as the foundation and industry as the leading factor," to achieve "modernization of industry, agriculture, science and technology and national defense." But increases in living standards can only be accomplished "gradually." "Socialist" forms of economic organization must develop "from lower to higher levels" and "from small to larger scale," with the Communes providing the basis for the ultimate "transition from collective ownership to ownership by the whole people." In foreign policy, "proletarian internationalism" must be upheld.

None of this is very surprising. But Mao then goes on to prescribe continuation for the indefinite future of many techniques of mass mobilization and ideological indoctrination which are distinctively Maoist and hark back to the days when leaders of the Chinese Communist Party were living in the caves of Yenan, struggling for power in the most primitive of conditions, not ruling a huge and increasingly complex society that is attempting to modernize and carry out the industrial and scientific revolutions.

The "mass line" must be continued, Mao says, "boldly to arouse the masses and to unfold mass movements on a large scale." The Party must rely in rural areas primarily upon "the poor and lower middle peasants." Ninety per cent of the people must be mobilized to struggle against the 10 per cent who are enemies. Unceasing ideological indoctrination must go on. "It is necessary to conduct extensive socialist education movements repeatedly in the cities and the countryside" involving "tit-for-tat struggles against the anti-socialist, capitalist and feudal forces—the landlords, rich peasants, counterrevolutionaries and bourgeois rightists, and the embezzlers, grafters and degenerates—in order to smash the attacks they unleash against socialism and to remold the majority of them into new men." The regime must nurture "a large detachment of working-class intellectuals who serve socialism and who are both 'red and expert'—i.e. who are both politically conscious and professionally competent," through continuing "cultural revolution." The three-pronged campaign to promote "class struggle, the struggle for production, and scientific experiment" must go on; "fierce class struggle" is required. Special efforts must be made to combat bureaucratism and prevent the growth of a privileged bureaucratic ruling group.

The most concrete proposals Mao makes are in many respects the most revealing about the sort of thing he believes to be necessary to continue the revolution. The gap between the salaries of all cadres, who work in the Party, government, enterprises, and Communes, and the income of the masses, must be reduced, presumably by a reduction of the cadres' salaries. The regime must maintain its "system of cadre participation in collective productive labor"—a program that since 1957 has sent millions of Party and non-Party bureaucrats to work in the countryside. It must also continue "the system under which officers serve as common soldiers at regu-

lar intervals"—a program started in 1958 which requires that all professional military officers spend time
every year living and working among the rank-and-
file conscriptees where, like ordinary privates, they are
expected to scrub pots and clean latrines. The program
to organize universal local militia must continue, to
make "everyone a soldier." And education should be
"combined with productive labor" so that all students
and intellectuals will become "habituated to manual
labor" and education will genuinely "serve proletarian
politics."

In an age of nuclear weapons, computers, and space
capsules, an age which China, however slowly, is
starting to enter, these prescriptions of Mao's for the
future sound oddly antiquarian. It seems evident, in
fact, that as the Maoist period in China approaches its
end, Mao himself is in many respects looking backward rather than forward. He would like to preserve—
or rather "restore"—the purity and integrity of the
revolutionary movement as it existed in its early years.
He insists that the Chinese Communists, as leaders of
a great state and modernizing nation, still continue to
use techniques of social and political action which they
evolved and found effective in earlier days and less
complicated situations.

Mao fears both the effects of time—which he sees
resulting in a slackening of revolutionary ardor and a
reemergence of traditional patterns of behavior—and
the social consequences of modernization—which

57

threaten to produce some form of revisionism. He seems hypnotized, in short, by what has been called "the Yenan complex," and does, indeed, seem to have become more and more of a "revolutionary romantic."

He clearly knows, however, that even in the Chinese Communist Party—and in its "higher leading organs" —there are men who now have different views, who are less influenced by political nostalgia, whose impulse is to look forward rather than backward, and who realize that as time passes and society changes the character of the revolution must change too. Mao fears that after he goes men of this stripe will lead Communist China in new directions, and he is now engaged in one final effort to do what he can to ensure that China keeps traveling what he considers to be the true and narrow path.

Mao's views on how the world revolution should develop in the future, and what China's relationship to it should be, appear to be—like his prescriptions for continuation of the revolution within China—essentially a projection of the Chinese Communist Party's past experience, and most particularly its experience during the halcyon days of Yenan.

The essential thesis of the article by Lin Piao on "people's war," which summarizes Mao's views on this subject, is that the Maoist model for revolution has now become the prime model for the world revolution as a whole. "Comrade Mao Tse-tung's theory of the establishment of rural revolutionary base areas and the encirclement of the cities from the countryside," Lin says, "is of outstanding and universal practical importance for the present revolutionary struggles of all the oppressed nations and peoples, and particularly for the revolutionary struggles of the oppressed nations and peoples in Asia, Africa, and Latin America against imperialism and its lackeys. . . . The basic political and economic conditions in many of these countries have many similarities to those that prevailed in old China. . . . The peasants constitute the main force of the national democratic revolution. . . . The countryside, and the countryside alone, can provide the revolutionary bases from which the revolutionaries can go forward to final victory."

Furthermore, Lin says, "Comrade Mao Tse-tung has formulated a complete theory of the new democratic revolution. He indicated that this revolution which is different from all others can only be, nay must be, a revolution against imperialism, feudalism, and bureaucratic capitalism. . . . Comrade Mao Tse-tung's theory of the new democratic revolution is the Marxist-Leninist theory of revolution by stages as well as the Marxist-Leninist theory of uninterrupted revolution."

Finally, Lin makes a dramatic statement in which he describes the world situation as a whole in terms of Mao's strategy. "Taking the entire globe, if North America and Western Europe can be called the 'cities of the world,' then Asia, Africa, and Latin America constitute 'the rural areas of the world.' . . . In the final analysis, the whole cause of world revolution hinges on the revolutionary struggles of the Asian, African, and Latin American peoples who make up the overwhelming majority of the world's population."

In short, this statement claims, in a way which must make Marx and Engels turn in their graves, that the crucial elements in the world revolution today are the underdeveloped nations and the peasants—not the industrial nations and urban proletariat. On this basis it puts forth a clear bid for worldwide Chinese leadership of the revolution and openly challenges the Soviet Union as well as the United States.

What are the essential ingredients for a successful Maoist-type revolution, as spelled out by Lin on the basis of Mao's past writings and statements? It requires several key elements: a strong, independent Communist Party, a broad Communist-led united front built on appeals to nationalism as well as social reform, a strong peasant base, and a revolutionary army which, by conducting protracted guerrilla and mobile warfare from rural "liberated areas," can ultimately "encircle the cities from the countryside."

Force and violence are essential. "Without a people's army the people have nothing," Lin says, quoting Mao. He goes on to say, "In the last analysis, the Marxist-Leninist theory of proletarian revolution is the theory of the seizure of state power by revolutionary violence. . . . Mao Tse-tung, using the simplest and most vivid language, advanced the famous thesis that 'political power grows out of the barrel of a gun.' He clearly pointed out: The seizure of power by armed force, the settlement of the issue by war, is the central task and highest form of revolution."

"People's war" must be "protracted war," involving a long "process of mobilizing, organizing, and arming the people." To succeed, a Communist Party, while maintaining its own independence, "must hold aloft the national banner, and, using the weapon of the united front, rally around itself the masses and the patriotic and anti-imperialist people who form more than ninety per cent of a country's population."

The people's army must of necessity be composed mainly of peasants, who are the "most reliable and the most numerous ally of the proletariat," the "main force" in the struggle. In fact, the struggle is "in essence a peasant revolutionary war." The army must combine "three military formations, that is, the regular forces, the local forces and the militia." It must be under firm Party control, since "politics is the commander, politics is the soul of everything." It must serve, simultaneously, as "a fighting force, a political work force, and a production corps." And when fighting, it must depend primarily on guerrilla warfare and secondarily on mobile warfare.

Rural bases are essential for the struggle. "In China, Lin says, "the work of building the revolutionary base areas was a grand rehearsal in preparation for nationwide victory. In these base areas, we built the Party, ran the organs of the state power, built the people's armed forces, and set up mass organizations; we engaged in industry and agriculture and operated cultural, educational and all other undertakings necessary for the independent existence of a separate region. Our base areas were in fact a State in miniature." In other words, these base areas make possible, as one Western scholar has put it, a "prefabricated revolution."

The tactics of struggle must be extremely flexible. "Comrade Mao Tse-tung enumerated the basic tactics of guerrilla warfare as follows: 'The enemy advances, we retreat; the enemy camps, we harass; the enemy tires, we attack; the enemy retreats, we pursue." Such flexibility must characterize every aspect of the struggle.

And "self-reliance" must be the foundation of every revolution. "Those countries which have won victory are duty-bound to support and aid the peoples who have not yet done so. Nevertheless, foreign aid can only play a supplementary role," and revolutionaries must "prepare to carry on the fight independently even when all material aid from the outside is cut off."

Consequently, there must be firm and unwavering faith that in the long run inferior power can overcome superior power. As Mao says, we must "despise the enemy strategically" even though we "take full account of him tactically," realizing that in the end "the imperialists and all reactionaries are paper tigers." "What is important primarily is not that which at any given moment seems to be durable and yet is already beginning to die away, but that which is arising and developing . . . [and] is invincible."

On a worldwide basis, the U.S. is the central enemy, and the "people of the world" should "form the broadest possible united front" to fight it. "At present, the main battlefield . . . is the vast area of Asia, Africa, and Latin America."

There should be no fear, such as the Soviet "revisionists" display, of the dangers of nuclear war. "The spiritual atom bomb which the revolutionary people possess is a far more powerful and useful weapon than the physical atom bomb. . . . The experience of innumerable revolutionary wars has borne out the truth that a revolutionary people who rise up with only their bare hands at the outset finally succeed in defeating ruling classes armed to the teeth."

All in all, this is a ringing statement of revolutionary faith which paints a grand vision of the future, with China in the center of it. While in the mid-1950's, "follow the path of the Russians" was a basic slogan in China, obviously what Peking is now proclaiming, in effect, is that the entire world should "follow the path of the Chinese."

But what, exactly, is the significance of the statement? It is certainly no "Mein Kampf," as some have suggested. It contains no blueprint of Chinese military expansionism. On the contrary, it stresses that every revolutionary group must, in a fundamental sense, be self-reliant, and it warns them not to expect the Chinese to fight their battles for them.

In essence, Lin Piao's article is a summary of Mao's diagnosis of forces at work in the world, rather than a design for expansionist Chinese action. China's role in the years ahead, as Mao sees it, will be to stimulate, encourage, advise, and lead revolutionaries everywhere, and he offers the Chinese Communist Party's revolutionary experience as the primary model for them to follow. But he does not advocate revolution abroad conducted by Chinese.

From Peking's viewpoint there are obviously many arguments that can be used to support this vision and to justify Mao's propositions. The Chinese Communists doubtless have a strong and genuine belief that their revolutionary experience is highly relevant to revolutionaries throughout the underdeveloped world, more relevant, certainly, than the Russian experience. They see a world where uprisings and revolts take place at frequent intervals in widely scattered areas, and with a high degree of ethnocentricity they tend to interpret them in the light of their own experience. There is ample evidence that many revolutionaries in many places are, in fact, fascinated by Mao's writings, especially those on guerrilla warfare, and are studying them assiduously.

In addition, because Peking now finds itself at odds with both of the two superpowers, it has good reason to emphasize a strategy that purports to turn weakness into strength. It recognizes that in terms of modern power, there is no prospect that it can soon achieve parity with these powers.[6] But at the same time it seems to believe, with considerable justification, that because the major powers are inhibited from using their nuclear weapons, conflicts can occur at a lower level of violence without necessarily leading to major war. Consequently, Mao, in one sense, sees the Chinese Communists' essential problem now to be similar to what it was during their struggle for power—namely, how to deal with more powerful adversaries from a position of relative weakness. His prescription, therefore, is also essentially the same: wear the enemy down gradually by conducting protracted revolutionary struggle.

But despite the seeming logic of such arguments, there are also strong arguments on the other side, and it is plausible to believe that they influence at least some leaders in Peking, even today. It is certainly possible that arguments against Mao's prescriptions could come increasingly to the fore after Mao's death. The Chinese Communist regime today represents not sim-

[6] Communist China has already set off four nuclear explosions, will soon develop a nuclear stockpile, and is perfecting its missile delivery systems, so that its nuclear capability may soon be a significant one. But there is no foreseeable prospect that Peking can achieve parity with Washington or Moscow in nuclear power. China's leaders seem to realize this and to view nuclear weapons primarily as a necessary deterrent to American and Soviet power and as an important instrument to enhance China's political influence.

ply a revolutionary movement but a modern state with complex interests which require normalized relations with a variety of other countries. Because of this fact, its actual policies, even now, are far more complicated than Lin's codification of Mao's faith in world revolution would suggest. The theory of people's war is essentially irrelevant to Peking's current policies toward Japan, Britain, or France—or even, for that matter, its existing policies toward Cambodia, the United Arab Republic, or Yemen. Many of Communist China's relationships with such countries are clearly based on Peking's pragmatic analysis of China's economic and other interests, even though they may be rationalized on the basis of the so-called theory of the intermediate zone, which, incidentally, is very different from the theory of people's wars and argues that virtually the entire world, including Europe and Japan, can and should cooperate in opposing the United States.

Conflict with both of the superpowers also involves obvious and serious costs and risks for China, and imposes basic limitations on its freedom of action. There have been many hints in Chinese Communist statements that at least some leaders in the regime—including P'eng Teh-huai who was purged as Minister of Defense in 1959—have questioned the wisdom of Mao's insistence on struggling with Moscow as well as Washington, and clearly some of them would favor a reduction of tensions in China's foreign relations, at least in relations with the Soviet Union.

Mao's Prescriptions for the Future

Finally, the evidence has mounted for some time that, because the main moving force in most of the underdeveloped world is nationalism rather than Communism, Peking's militant revolutionary posture has tended to be counterproductive and to produce negative reactions even in this region.

The setbacks that Communist China has encountered over the past year and a half at the Algiers Conference and in Indonesia, Ghana, and elsewhere must have convinced some leaders in Peking that if they are really to "combine theory and practice," changes in their tactics, or possibly even their strategy, are called for.

Mao's theories of "people's war," therefore, are not now, and are not likely to be in the future, an adequate basis for operationally feasible foreign policies that can meet Peking's needs and defend its interests as a modern power. They, like Mao's formulas for continuing revolution at home, seem to be, in many respects, primarily an expression of Mao's "revolutionary romanticism" which looks to the past more than to the future.

In sum, Mao's prescriptions for the future, both at home and abroad, suggest that in many ways what Mao stands for is obsolete as a guide to action for China as it moves along the road toward modernization and increasingly plays the role of a great power. Maoism has served the Chinese Communists well in the past, but its utility will decrease steadily in the future.

Mao's Prescriptions for the Future

Ideology will doubtless continue to be important; it is needed as cement to help ensure the unity of the regime and society. But its content is not likely to survive unchanged. This does not mean, of course, that Mao's advice will automatically be rejected after his death. Although the possibility of "de-Maoization" cannot be ruled out, Mao's immediate successors may try, self-consciously, to clothe themselves in Maoist garments, in order to prove that they are the legitimate "heirs of the revolution." But what seems likely is that under Mao's successors, the fact will become even clearer than it is now that Yenan-type measures to preserve outdated revolutionary traditions, and heroic proselyting for "people's wars" abroad, will not adequately serve the needs and interests of a modernizing great power.

What seems likely is that even if Peking's leaders continue to give lip service to Mao's admonitions on "how to carry the revolution on to the end," in practice both Maoism and the nature of the revolution in China will eventually undergo many changes—in the directions which Mao, quite justifiably, now fears. This may not occur immediately after Mao's death, but in the post-Mao era there will be many forces working for change in China, and their effects will be felt in time.

CHAPTER III

The Succession and Generational Change

THE WINDS of change are blowing in Communist China. Turbulence is not, of course, something new. In fact, Peking's leaders view the essence of the revolutionary process as being "like the waves of the sea," an inevitable succession of contrasting periods, alternately calm and turbulent. But what is now taking place is more than simply a repetition of past upheavals, and the Chinese Communists themselves seem to realize that the current turbulence marks the start of a new stage in the Chinese revolution, one different from any they have experienced in the past. In a basic sense they will soon be traveling uncharted seas.

As I have tried to suggest earlier, the uncertainties about the future arise in part from fundamental ideological and policy dilemmas, and from the prospect of mounting pressures to solve basic problems, such as how best to push forward the developmental process in China, to sustain a sense of revolutionary momentum, to adapt revolutionary techniques of social mobilization to a society striving for modernization, and to apply Maoist principles under conditions very different from those out of which they evolved.

However, perhaps the greatest uncertainties arise from the prospect of major changes in leadership, for not only Mao himself but the entire first generation of Chinese Communist leaders will start to pass from the scene before very long.

It is not surprising that this prospect raises many unanswered questions. Mao has personally guided the Chinese Communist Party for over 30 years, and no one really knows how the character of the regime will change when he dies. Moreover, to a startling degree, the other leaders who rule China today—not only in the national capital but also in the provinces and even in the counties—belong to the group which assumed power immediately after 1949. They are a known and tested group, but they are aging, and being mortal they will begin to disappear before long. The prospect of such change inevitably beclouds the future.

The average age of the men who belonged to the Chinese Communist Politburo at the start of this year—before the current purge—was approaching 70. To be specific, its regular members averaged almost 67; the alternate members were only slightly younger, averaging 63. The median age of the entire Central Committee is over 60. Ministers in the Peking government average 62 years of age, and the average age of Provincial Party Secretaries and Governors is close to 60.

Moreover, in recent years the age of men holding such posts has kept steadily rising. In the decade between 1955 and 1965, the average age of Provincial

Succession and Generational Change

Party Secretaries and Governors rose by nine years, and that of Ministers by six years.

Even at the county level, the information available from a few specific localities indicates that members of the take-over group of local Party chiefs have clung to, and aged in, their offices. All of this means that one can say, with actuarial certainty, that before very long a large portion of the top leadership group in China will begin to pass from the scene, with results that will be felt at every level of the country.

What impact will the coming succession and period of generational change in the leadership have on the Chinese Communist regime? Unfortunately, the social sciences do not provide their practitioners with crystal balls enabling them to make confident predictions about the future, even for countries such as ours where the data are inexhaustible; the variables in dynamic social situations are simply too numerous. In the case of China, the information available is fragmentary, at best. Nevertheless, it is possible, by examining facts that are known about the present leadership group in Communist China, and by analyzing trends in the structure and characteristics of China's elite that now seem to be under way, to speculate—hopefully in an informed fashion—about possible developments in the future and their conceivable significance—both for Communist China itself and for other nations, including our own, which will have to deal with the next generation of Chinese leaders for a long time to come.

Succession and Generational Change

The first generation of top revolutionary leaders in Communist China consists of a very remarkable group of men. They all proved themselves as leaders during the long struggle for power, a struggle in which only the fittest survived. They have demonstrated time and again that they are competent, dedicated, and tough-minded revolutionaries, and they now have many years of experience behind them. They have also shown a striking degree of unity and common purpose, which—until recently—has been a major source of strength to the Chinese Communist regime.

Those holding the very top leadership posts, not only in the political system but also in society as a whole, are relatively easy to identify. In contrast to the situation in pluralistic societies, where the channels to membership in the top elite are varied and the elite's composition is sometimes difficult to define precisely, in Communist China, as in other Communist-ruled countries, membership in the top elite generally coincides with membership in the Communist Party Central Committee. One's ranking in this group, moreover, is usually a fairly accurate index of power, influence, and prestige. Power relationships obviously change over time, and between sessions of the Party Congresses—which elect the members of the Central Committee—it is not always wholly clear who may have risen within the Party apparatus to top leadership status. Nevertheless, the Central Committee's roster can clearly be regarded as the main indication of membership in the top elite.

In China, the continuity and stability of this group has been exceptional. Apart from the very few who have died or been purged, the Central Committee members elected by the Seventh Party Congress in 1945 still constitute the core of the group and generally hold the top positions in the rank list. The Committee was significantly expanded by the Eighth Party Congress sessions in 1956 and 1958, but for the most part the new members elected in those years were simply additions to the group, not substitutions for earlier members, and they generally now occupy lower positions in the rankings.

At present 179 regular and alternate members of the Central Committee are living and active. To discover the characteristics of the top leaders in China, therefore, one must examine the backgrounds of the men—and the few women—belonging to this group. In operational terms, there are subgroups under the Committee that dominate policy-making. In general the Central Committee functions as a ratifying body rather than a decision-making institution; key policy decisions have generally been made either by the twenty-odd member Politburo, by its seven-man Standing Committee, or by Mao himself. Nevertheless, all members in good standing of the Central Committee occupy posts of great power and authority throughout society. They are a fairly homogeneous group in many respects.

And their characteristics reveal, therefore, the nature of the top ruling elite in general.

In social origin, a large majority of the Central Committee's members came from middle or even upper-class backgrounds. Typically, their fathers were middle or rich peasants, landlords, merchants, or officials. Only a small number came from families of poor peasants or urban workers. In some respects, therefore, their characteristics, at least in terms of social origin, do not seem radically different from those of the Kuomintang leaders whom they replaced, although more of the Communists came from rural backgrounds, and this clearly contributed to the strength of their rural orientation by comparison with their predecessors. But similarities of this sort with past leaders are of limited significance. The outlook and experience of these men, acquired over the years, has made them very different from those who preceded them.

In general, they are a well-educated group. Close to three-quarters of those at the top had some exposure to "higher education," in colleges, normal schools, universities, or military academies, either in China or abroad, and only a small minority had no formal education. This fact places them in the mainstream of history in China, where education has always been closely associated with political power. It sets them apart from the masses of ordinary Chinese, and in fact from many lower-ranking leaders in the Chinese

Communist Party. The Party still includes large numbers of cadres recruited from the poor peasantry during the struggle for power, and many of these uneducated ex-peasants still occupy powerful positions at all levels in the political apparatus in Communist China. But very few men who have lacked education have been able to rise to the very top level of leadership represented in the Central Committee.

Foreign education or training of some sort is also a common characteristic of many of the leading Party elders. In fact, well over half of the Central Committee regulars elected in 1945, who now dominate the top of the rank list, had some education abroad. The largest number went to the Soviet Union, but significant numbers spent time in Western Europe or in Japan.

Whatever their social origin or education, however, in a fundamental sense these are "self-made men," most of whom, if they had to fill out forms requiring a statement about their early careers, would have to write simply "professional revolutionary." Apart from those who were military men before joining the revolutionary movement, most entered the Party when they were very young, and few had had previous professional careers. "Party life" and "revolutionary struggle" were the essence, therefore, of their early career experience.

For most of these men the main channels for career advancement after they joined the Party were

Party organizational work and service in the Party's revolutionary army. Because the Chinese revolution from the late 1920's on was—to use the Communists' own phrase—one of "armed revolution against armed counterrevolution," a majority of those who rose to the top had active military experience, either as commanders or political commissars. This was true, for example, of about two-thirds of the leaders elected to the Central Committee in 1945. Subsequently, the proportion of men at the top who have had active military careers has declined, but it is still sizeable, and military experience has had a strong influence on the entire outlook of the Party.

The skills which members of the top leadership group developed prior to achieving power were mainly, therefore, those of military combat, political organization, and ideological mobilization, rather than technical or professional skills of other sorts. In the 17 years since 1949, many have developed other specialized skills, or have at least become identified with fields of activity in which professional and technical concerns are important, but as a group this first generation of leaders has tended to idealize revolutionary generalists rather than professional specialists.

Their patterns of political action, and what they like to call their "working style," still very much reflect their earlier experiences and lines of career development. The "mass line," stressing revolutionary techniques of indoctrination and mobilization, is rooted in their past, and the dominant leaders insist that such techniques must be continued in the present and future.

Geographically, a high percentage of the present top leadership group comes from central China, especially from Mao's own province of Hunan and the neighboring provinces of Szechwan, Hupeh, and Kiangsi. This does not reflect regionalism of a traditional sort, which the Party has consciously tried to suppress. But it does reflect the continuing importance of personal ties, as well as the simple fact that it was in the central provinces that the Chinese Communists' revolutionary struggle achieved its first successes under Mao's leadership.

The unity and cohesion of this group has been almost unique in the history of major revolutionary regimes. The acceptance of a common ideology and agreement on basic goals provide part of the explanation, but not a sufficient explanation. Many other revolutionary groups have been fractured by internal struggles soon after achieving power, despite the cement of ideology and common objectives.

The shared experience of fighting a prolonged revolutionary struggle, successfully, obviously contributed to the cohesiveness of this group. Not only did all of the present members of the Chinese Communist Central Committee join the Party before it achieved power; virtually all had 25 years or more of experience in the Party before being accepted into the top elite. A great many "old school ties," dating to the 1920's and 1930's, created strong bonds among them. These included participation in the Nanchang Uprising of 1927, in the Kiangsi Soviet in the early 1930's, in the Long March to the northwest in the mid-1930's, and in the Yenan regime during the Sino-Japanese War.

Mao Tse-tung's personal leadership and dominating role have also been major factors for unity. We do not really know very much about patterns of decision-making at the highest levels in Communist China, but Mao's role has been crucial. It appears that Mao, from his dominating position, has put great stress on the need for reaching a consensus, under his own leadership. It also appears that by and large he has been remarkably successful in preventing internal tensions and disputes from developing into disruptive factionalism.

In a sense, therefore, collective leadership of a sort appears to have operated at the very highest levels. But Mao has been the kingpin, and his leadership has been all-important. The available evidence suggests that on numerous occasions in the period since 1949, debate on key issues has been halted (at least temporarily) when Mao himself made the crucial policy decisions—such as those on collectivization and, later, on the Great Leap Forward and communization. The dominant role which Mao has played in the past obviously highlights the question of what will happen when he dies.

Another explanation for the cohesiveness of the top

leadership in China has been the effectiveness of the distinctive techniques which the Chinese Communists have evolved over the years for managing internal tensions and promoting ideological unity and organizational discipline. From 1921 until 1935 the Party was wracked by internal factionalism and purges, but since Mao's rise to power in 1935, not only has the purge rate been relatively low, the techniques of Party purging have generally been nonviolent.

After the ouster of Chang Kuo-t'ao in 1938, the only major figures of Politburo rank who were subsequently purged—until the purge of this year, which will be discussed later—were Kao Kang and Jao Shu-shih[1] in 1954 and P'eng Teh-huai in 1959. Both the 1954 and 1959 purges were of major importance, and the consequences of the latter are, in fact, still affecting the situation in China. Nevertheless, one can say that by comparison with the record of other totalitarian regimes such as the one in the Soviet Union, the Chinese Communists have maintained a degree of top-level unity that is truly phenomenal. Moreover, of the victims of purges mentioned, only Kao Kang—who reportedly committed suicide—is known to be dead; P'eng Teh-huai, actually, continued to be listed as a Politburo member even after he disappeared into some unknown limbo in 1959.

The Chinese Communists' basic approach to man-

[1] Jao Shu-shih was not actually a Politburo member but was doubtless close to achieving such status.

79

aging internal tensions is one that they call "cheng feng," or rectification. Since the original rectification campaign of 1942-44, the Party has organized such campaigns at frequent intervals. Each has been an intensive effort to reindoctrinate all Party members and tighten discipline. Although such campaigns have resulted in many demotions and expulsions, they have not involved widespread physical liquidation of errant members. As Mao has put it, the aim has been to treat the illness and cure the patient.

An extensive literature has developed on how to manage "inner Party struggle"—including a volume with this title by Liu Shao-ch'i. In these writings the Party leaders have recognized that internal struggle of a sort within the Party is inevitable, and even desirable, but they have insisted that only "principled struggle" on ideological and policy issues is permissible, and they have tried to suppress all factional struggles for power. The leaders assert that all inner Party debate must lead to the formulation of policies which once defined must then be accepted by all.

In practice, there clearly has been much debate on policy within the Party. There is reason to believe, moreover, that under the façade of seemingly monolithic unity, there are doubtless many significant informal groupings, based on shared views on policy as well as personal ties. But there has been very little evidence in the past of clear-cut factions struggling for power within the Chinese Communist Party.

Succession and Generational Change

The men who make up the top Party elite in China have controlled, ever since 1949, every organizational sector of Chinese society—the government, army, and mass organizations, as well as the Party apparatus itself—through an all-embracing system of interlocking directorates. In China, the role of the Communist Party seems to have been even more dominant, in fact, than in most other Communist-ruled societies, not only at the top but at all levels, and Party units embedded in virtually every institution and locality in the country have ensured that the top elite could make its will prevail.

Despite the stability and continuity of China's top leadership since 1949, however, the characteristics of the nation's elite have not remained static. Changes of many sorts have taken place over time. In looking toward the future, therefore, it is important to examine recent trends, identify emerging problems, and get some sense of the directions in which change seems to be pointing. A number of important trends are worth noting. Not all of them can be documented in great detail, but they are at least suggested by the limited evidence available.

The most obvious and one of the most important trends is the one that I have stressed already, namely the rising age level of the leadership. The continuity of the leadership at all levels indicates, of course, that the rate of upward mobility within the elite has been low. This was not true during the regime's early years.

Succession and Generational Change

At the time of Communist takeover, there was a massive displacement of leaders from the old regime, and for a while there was a rapid expansion of governmental activities and institutions, so that opportunities for advancement at all levels were good. However, by the late 1950's there seemed to be, if anything, more downward than upward mobility within the entire elite group. As a result of the regime's efforts to decentralize many of its activities, and retrench at the center, millions of men and women were actually "transferred downward" to lower-level jobs, especially in rural areas. The expansion of the Central Committee in 1956 and 1958 did, it is true, involve upward movement for a few men in the highest echelons of leadership (for those involved it was really little more than recognition of positions already achieved), but most members of the elite have found the opportunities to move upward in the hierarchy strictly limited since the 1950's because older, established Party leaders have held tenaciously to their posts and their power.

In short, the regime has really failed, so far, to evolve effective means to superannuate aging leaders, or to ensure processes of upward mobility and infuse new blood into leadership positions. Consequently, the stability of the leadership, which was clearly an important source of strength in earlier years, has increasingly become a source of potential weakness. Able Party members at lower levels have been frustrated by the lack of opportunities to move to the top, and this frustration has created latent pressure upward, which is likely to become increasingly important when structural changes at the top begin to take place, probably soon after the death or removal of key top leaders.

There has been, in other words, a real and growing generational gap between older and younger cadres within the elite in China. As the gap has become more obvious, moreover, many Party leaders appear to have become, if anything, less confident of the reliability of younger cadres, especially those who have joined since 1949, and increasingly reluctant to turn over power to them.

Since the Tenth Party Central Committee Plenum in late 1962, there has been much talk of training "revolutionary successors," and early this year a campaign to "revolutionize" Party Committees at the county level resulted in reorganizational steps in many counties, which may have begun to push some younger cadres to the fore. However, not surprisingly, men who have exercised power for many years do not easily relinquish it. At some point more dramatic steps will probably be necessary to bring younger men into leadership positions.

Such men may not have to wait until the entire first generation passes from the scene. Whether the current Red Guards campaign, with its accent on youth, will have this result remains to be seen. In any case, it seems likely that as changes in power relationships occur at the center, these may be reflected increasingly at lower levels. It would not be surprising if competing top leaders attempted to build grass-roots support by allying with and replacing present incumbents of key local posts by new men, many of whom could be ambitious younger cadres who have been restricted in their advancement opportunities in the past.

Another trend in recent years, which I mentioned earlier, has been the growth of an increasingly complex system of social stratification among the elite at all levels. Both the reemergence of old patterns of Chinese bureaucratic behavior and pressures toward administrative regularization and routinization have contributed to this trend.

At present, throughout the bureaucracy in China, including the Party apparatus itself, there is an intense rank-consciousness, which is a far cry from the Party's revolutionary ideals. Party members now are not only categorized by salary and job level but are also ranked informally by seniority in the Party. In practice seniority has been of crucial importance in determining prestige and position.

A great point is made of the differences between "old cadres" and "new cadres"—with the year 1949 generally taken as the dividing line between them— and even the "old cadres" are divided into a large number of subcategories based on seniority, each of which has a different label. For example, old Party members are labeled "Long March cadres" if they participated in that epic trek, "Yenan" or "Anti-Japanese

War cadres" if they participated in the struggle from the mid-1930's to the mid-1940's, and "Liberation War cadres" if they joined the revolutionary struggle in its final stage between 1945 and 1949. Most top Party leaders at all levels in society are still persons who belong to one or another of these categories of "old cadres," and in general the greater one's seniority, the greater one's prestige and power.

The Party's top leaders—above all, Mao himself—appear to be genuinely determined to fight against bureaucratization in all of its forms, but their efforts to date have not been very effective in combating bureaucratic rank-consciousness of this sort. In fact, their own tendency to stress the reliability and trustworthiness of "old cadres" over relative newcomers has been a major cause of the trend.

Eventually, however, there may be a strong counter-reaction, when new and younger leaders demand that ability, rather than rankings based on seniority, should be the primary basis for advancement. The enthusiasm with which many young people have participated in recent Red Guards' activities—which clearly have been designed to shake up the Party bureaucracy as well as to combat "feudal" and "bourgeois" attitudes among the general population—may be in part because of the gap that has steadily grown between the well-entrenched old cadres in the regime and the youth.

Trends toward bureaucratization and routinization seem likely to grow, nevertheless. Mass campaigns such as those now under way in China can probably do no more than check them temporarily. And even a large infusion of new blood into the bureaucracy would probably not halt such trends.

The dominance of the Party's role in China, in the society as a whole as well as in political life, has varied over time since 1949, but it has always been very great indeed. Party positions clearly confer greater power and prestige than government posts of roughly equivalent status; for example, Provincial Party First Secretaries are obviously more powerful and respected than Provincial Governors. Those most ambitious for power have tended, therefore, to be drawn into the Party apparatus.

In the late 1950's, moreover, direct Party control over every sector of society was reasserted in an extreme form, and Party leaders at every level became increasingly involved in direct management of the society instead of simply supervising others. The retreat from extremism in the post-Great Leap period reduced the role of the Party somewhat, but more recently, in the process of political radicalization that has taken place since late 1962, the tendency for the Party to assert its dominance has become evident again—although now the increasing role of military leaders in Chinese national life may have checked this trend to some extent.

The insistence on Party primacy has inhibited, in the past, the emergence in China of strong parallel bureaucracies independent of Party control, in the army, police, civil government agencies, and economic enterprises. But it is questionable whether this situation will continue indefinitely, and it may already be changing. Not only has tension grown between the professional experts and Party organization men throughout society (within the army, economic enterprises, and other institutions), but recent events suggest that while the central Party apparatus is still a power center of crucial importance, other centers of power—especially, today, the military establishment—have become increasingly important.

Within the Party itself, moreover, there appears to have been a steady trend over the years toward the development of specialized interests and functional differentiation. This trend obviously runs counter to the idealized goal of a fairly homogenized Party composed of dedicated revolutionary generalists.

Today, most institutions and cadres in China are grouped into what the Chinese Communists call "hsi t'ung" or "systems," which are vertically organized functional groupings of agencies operating on a nationwide basis. These "systems" cover such areas as political and legal affairs, propaganda and education, finance and trade, and industry and communications, and each of the major ones is supervised by a Department in the Party Central Committee, as well as by a Staff Office under the State Council. A great many cadres already tend to identify themselves with a particular "system," and there is good reason to believe that over time Party members are likely to identify themselves increasingly with these functionally defined fields.

This trend suggests that within the Party itself there are now—and are likely to be increasingly in the future—men at all levels, from top to bottom, whose major preoccupation is with certain specialized tasks. Because of this, varying outlooks and conflicts of needs, priorities, and even goals between men working in different fields are likely to become steadily more important in the political process in China.

Conflicts of interest between the authorities at the center of national power and those in the country's large regions and provinces are also very real in China and may well become increasingly important. There has been a constant interplay, in fact, over the past 17 years between national and regional forces, and between pressures working for either centralization or decentralization. In crude terms one can say that at the time of takeover the regime tolerated a fairly high degree of decentralization; in the early 1950's it emphasized the desirability of fairly extreme centralization; in the latter 1950's it moved toward extreme decentralization; and since the end of the Great Leap, while the trend has again been toward centralization, there now appears to be more of a balance than in the past.

Today, even though a majority of the top leaders in the regions and provinces in China are members of the Party Central Committee, close to three-quarters of all Central Committee members are based in the national capital. This contrasts with the situation during the regime's early years, when two-thirds of the leaders of Central Committee rank lived and worked at the regional or provincial level. Nevertheless, leadership at the regional or provincial level still can be, and often is, an important springboard to power at the top, the most notable recent examples of this being the cases of T'ao Chu and Li Hsueh-feng, who jumped to positions of great power at the center this year from positions as Party First Secretaries in the Central-South and North China regions.

By and large the central Party apparatus in China has maintained very effective control over local centers of power, and it has acted strongly to suppress any real or potential threats to central control, as in the case of Kao Kang in 1954. Since the decentralization of the late 1950's, however, the importance of the provinces as bases of political power appears to have increased. During the Great Leap, the power of local Party leaders expanded enormously; since then their authority has been reduced, but regional and provincial posts still provide many opportunities for able and ambitious Party leaders to build national influence. In addition to the cases of T'ao Chu and Li Hsueh-feng, already noted, the recent evidence that P'eng Chen— the most prominent victim of the current purge—used the Peking Party machine as a major prop for his power and was attacked by organs of the Shanghai Party apparatus acting under Mao's instructions, throws new light on the importance of regional power bases.

Looking to the future, if the processes of change in China result in at least some diffusion of power at the center, as seems probable, there is a possibility that provincial-based leaders could play a more important role in the overall political picture. This does not mean that provincial localism of an old-fashioned sort is likely soon to emerge; the central authorities will doubtless continue to act strongly to suppress overt challenges from persons operating from local bases of power. But political links with strong regional leaders could become increasingly important to competing figures at the center of national power, and ambitious regional leaders may increasingly find opportunities to use their local power to enhance their national influence.

At the center of national decision-making in China, the institutional bases for individual power are likely to become increasingly important, and increasingly competitive in many respects, in the years ahead, particularly after the death of Mao. This means that top leaders who have their roots in particular institutional hierarchies, such as the Party apparatus, the army, the government bureaucracy, the Public Security apparatus, or the propaganda machine, may well use their own power bases, more than in the past, to strengthen their national influence; conversely, they may increasingly use their national influence to protect and strengthen their own particular institutional bases of power.

Mao's idealized conception of how the process of decision-making should operate at the center of power in China calls for the top leaders, under his personal leadership, to subordinate their special interests and view problems in a broad perspective, deciding what is "good for the revolution" in a general sense.

In practice, however, the highest decision-making bodies in Communist China have generally been representative, even in the past, of the major institutional interests in the nation. This has been the case, for example, even in the seven-man Standing Committee of the Politburo, which possesses ultimate decision-making power in China. Apart from Mao himself, who has stood above any special interests within the regime, most of the others have tended to become identified primarily with one particular sector of the political system.

Liu Shao-ch'i rose to prominence through Party organizational work—although after becoming Chairman of the government in 1959 he, like Mao, may have become less identified with any particular sector. Chou En-lai, China's Premier, is clearly identified with the government bureaucracy. At the age of 80, Chu Teh is now a fairly inactive Party elder, but even though he was formerly a Vice-Chairman of the government and now heads the Standing Committee of the National People's Congress, his background identifies him mainly with the military establishment. Ch'en Yun, who disappeared from view at the time of the Great Leap—apparently because of his disapproval of the Leap policies—and only recently reappeared, is clearly identified with the government bureaucracy, particularly with the economic agencies of government. Lin Piao, Minister of Defense, is clearly identified with the military establishment, and Teng Hsiao-p'ing, General Secretary of the Party, with the Party apparatus. In a similar fashion, many if not most of the other members of the Politburo now tend to be identified primarily with one or another primary institutional base.

Undoubtedly, even in a Politburo dominated by Mao, particular institutional interests have influenced the way in which these men have functioned in the Party's highest decision-making bodies. Nevertheless, Mao's insistence that leaders of this sort should rise above their specialized preoccupations and dedicate themselves to the general good has greatly influenced the regime, and under his leadership factional struggles, based on conflicting institutional interests, appear to have been kept to a minimum.

In the future, however, and particularly after Mao dies, conflicting institutional interests are likely to become increasingly important and competitive and to have a greater influence on the policy-making process, even at the highest levels.

Trends in this direction are already evident, but today the relative positions and influence of different institutional sectors seem to be in flux. Consequently, it is extremely difficult to know what the real balance between them is, at present, or to estimate how power relationships among them are likely to evolve in the future.

Until recently, it appeared that the Party apparatus, run by the Secretariat under Teng Hsiao-p'ing, had been rising steadily in importance. Before the shifts resulting from the current purge, the Secretariat's ten regular and three alternate members included seven Politburo members, and all the rest belonged to the Central Committee. In some respects, although in theory the Secretariat is not a policy-making body, in practice it and the Party Departments under it have obviously played a very significant role affecting policy in the course of supervising the day-to-day operations of the Party.[2]

As its importance has grown, the Secretariat, like other top bodies, has tended increasingly to become representative of various institutional interests in the regime. Hence it cannot be regarded simply as a body promoting the views of those whose interests are identified with the Party apparatus alone. Nevertheless, there is little doubt that it has provided the primary power base of men such as Teng who are Party organi-

[2] In the current upheaval, the three most prominent victims to date (P'eng Chen, Lu Ting-yi, and Lo Jui-ch'ing) were all members of the Secretariat, and three rising figures (T'ao Chu, Liu Ning-yi, and Yeh Chien-ying) have recently been appointed to it.

zation men par excellence and who regard the Party apparatus as the key center of power in the regime. Organization men of this sort have dominated personnel policies throughout much of the regime, in the government as well as the Party, and this has enabled them to wield great power.

In the past few months, however, Teng and the Party organization men have been overshadowed—at least temporarily—by Lin Piao's meteoric rise. The growing national importance of the army, and of military men in general, has been, in fact, one of the most striking recent trends. As stated earlier, since the purge of P'eng Teh-huai in 1959, Party control over the army has been strongly reasserted, indoctrination in Maoist principles has been intensively pushed, and the "professionals" have been subjected to attack. But at the same time the broader national role of the army as a whole has steadily grown.

Ever since the Tenth Party Plenum in 1962, the army has been glorified in an unprecedented way as the model for all of society, and recently a growing number of military men have been assigned important posts in civilian agencies—for example, as heads of ministries as well as political commissars in many economic institutions.

Finally, in mid-August of 1966, Lin Piao, China's top military leader, emerged as Mao's newly designated heir. Lin is now credited with having "creatively applied" Maoist principles, an encomium not granted casually. He stands next to Mao whenever the two men attend public or ceremonial functions. And posters have appeared proclaiming "Long Live Chairman Mao! Long Live Lin Piao!" Clearly, he has supplanted Liu Shao-ch'i as the second-ranking leader in Peking with Mao's support.

Apparently, Mao has turned to Lin Piao and the military because he believes that they will most effectively propagate the ideals of disciplined mass action which Mao thinks are necessary for society as a whole. Perhaps Mao also believes that in the approaching transitional period, after his death, military control will be essential to ensure stability. It is also possible that the military establishment itself, or at least Lin and the others now dominating it, has demanded greater power and influence. Whatever the explanation, the recent growth of the influence of the military has been remarkable.

Another important trend that has been visible for some years has been the increasing importance of the regime's specialists in political control—including both the policemen and the propagandists. In the late 1950's, the Public Security apparatus broadly expanded its authority, asserting control over the judiciary and procuracy. An increasing number of persons with Public Security backgrounds were appointed to important positions. At the local level, it appears from refugees' accounts that Public Security agencies have exerted a pervasive and growing influence in recent years. Symbolic of this general trend was the rapid rise of Lo Jui-ch'ing, the nation's top policeman, who was promoted in 1959 to a Vice Premiership and, after many years as Minister of Public Security, became Chief of Staff of the People's Liberation Army.

During this same period, the regime's propagandists also seemed to play a role of increasing importance at all levels, since they were in charge of the intensified rectification and mass indoctrination programs that developed after the Tenth Plenum. In 1965, the nation's top propagandist, Lu Ting-yi, who headed the Party's Propaganda Department, was appointed Minister of Culture as well.

In the current purge, however, both Lo and Lu have been ousted from their major posts. The reasons are still obscure, but the most plausible explanation for their fall is that they were becoming too powerful, and that together with P'eng Chen they challenged the policies and positions of Mao and those at the very top.

In recent months, large numbers of lesser figures in the propaganda field have been purged, and it would not be surprising if many of those in the Public Security apparatus who have been associated with Lo have also suffered.

This does not necessarily mean, however, that the police and propaganda agencies, as such, will decline in importance. In fact, because they are responsible for vital control functions, their importance may grow during a period of transition in the top leadership. What is clear, though, is that the men aspiring to supremacy, in the struggle to succeed Mao, must try to ensure that the regime's policemen and propagandists give them full support; any challenges from them are dangerous.

One would naturally expect that the recent trends toward political radicalization and the growing emphasis on military, political, and ideological control would adversely affect the position of China's administrators, planners, and technical bureaucrats. And in some respects this has been the case. These men do not control the vital power centers in the regime, and they are not in a position to compete for supreme authority.

It is significant, however, that men of this sort still hold very influential positions, and to date none has been victimized in the current purge. Moreover, as stated earlier, the continuation so far of fairly reasonable, pragmatic, and moderate economic policies suggests that they seem to have been able to exert a significant influence on policy, even though they have not controlled the most powerful instruments of coercive political power.

Li Fu-ch'un, Chairman of the State Planning Commission, and Li Hsien-nien, Minister of Finance, continue to be prominent members of the Party's Secretariat as well as being members of the Politburo. Po Yi-po, Chairman of the State Economic Commission, has retained his position as an alternative Politburo member. And Ch'en Yun has suddenly reappeared after eight years of total eclipse.

It does not seem likely that men of this sort can hope to achieve political supremacy, at least in the foreseeable future. However, because they bear primary responsibility for economic activities that are essential to the achievement of the regime's developmental goals, the top political leaders, whoever they are, can ill afford to ignore them or to disregard their advice. How much influence they will be able to exert in the period immediately ahead will obviously depend in part on the major policy decisions made by the dominant leadership. But because they are really indispensable, their influence on policy may well be greater than their political power. Even if the top positions of power continue to elude them, and the dominant leaders propagate the virtues of Maoist methods of indoctrination and mobilization, these men may have some success in insisting on a more pragmatic approach to China's problems. In some respects, as was suggested earlier, this seems to be the situation today.

A number of other trends in the leadership group in China are also worth noting.

One is a steady shift in the locus of the geographical origins of the leadership. The dominance of persons from Central China persists, and will as long as the present Party elders live. But the rising generation of second-level leaders will be heavily weighted in favor of men from North China—the Party's main area of expansion in the late 1930's and early 1940's. In time, representation from other regions may also increase, but less dramatically. Leaders from Northeast China suffered following the purge of Kao Kang, and there still appear to be relatively few rising stars in the Party from South China, the region that was "liberated" last, or the Yangtze Valley, which was Chiang Kai-shek's base of power. The coming shift in the geographical center of gravity of the leadership will probably occur fairly gradually, and it is not likely to result in any obvious regional identification of the Party, any more than the concentration of first generation leaders from Central China did. But it does mean that the coming generation of leaders will have many personal and local ties that are different from those of the men now in power—a fact that will highlight the process of generational change.

Another trend worth noting has been the steady increase in recent years of the number of men holding second-level jobs as Party Secretaries or Vice Ministers in Party and government agencies throughout the regime. Many future leaders may emerge from this group. The number of Vice Ministers has doubled in the last decade, and Provincial Party Secretaries (holding jobs under the First Secretaries) and Deputy Governors have also multiplied. One suspects that in some instances, particularly in certain central agencies, men placed in these second-rank posts have played an increasingly important role in the actual running of their institutions, and it is plausible to believe that trends toward functional specialization may have affected them more than some of their aging superiors. Relatively little is known about these men, but it is clear that they constitute one important reservoir from which top leaders will increasingly be drawn as older leaders pass from the scene.

Still another trend in recent years has been a slow but steady rise in the purge rate in China. Only this year has the trend seemed dramatic. But it was apparent earlier. In fact, ever since the crucial period of 1957-1958—the period of the "100 flowers," the rectification movement, the anti-Rightist campaign, the Great Leap, and communization—the regime has found it necessary to demote or expel a significantly larger number of influential leaders than in earlier years; it has, however, continued to rely primarily on nonviolent means to do so.[3]

The cyclical alternation of periods of tension and relaxation that has characterized the process of social change in Communist China ever since 1949 does not, in and of itself, seem to provide a sufficient explanation for this trend. Rather it may well by symptomatic of a gradual weakening of consensus, and a steady growth in China not only of ideological and policy differences

[3] According to Donald W. Klein, of the 179 living members of the Central Committee, approximately 25 are now politically "out" (that is, purged or forced into inactivity, or greatly reduced in influence), so that the figure for active and "effective" Central Committee members now appears to be about 150.

but also of conflicting group interests—trends that seem likely to develop further in the future.

The steady growth of differences on policy questions relating to economic, political, intellectual, military, and foreign policy matters is one important reason why the coming post-Mao period is likely to be very different in many respects from the initial period of Communist rule in China.

Many statements made during the purge this year indicate that ever since the failures of the Great Leap, and the ensuing purge of "Rightists" in 1959, there has been continuing, and apparently mounting, debate in China, most of it behind the scenes, on a wide range of issues. Moreover, while clear-cut factions have been impossible to identify, the evidence suggests that particular leaders have tended to be identified with certain outlooks and policy positions, that personal ties between leaders have been important, as always in China, and that significant groupings have tended to emerge, probably based both on policy preferences and on personal associations.

While many issues have been involved, there seems to have been a polarization, based on the kinds of problems and questions which I discussed earlier, into leftists and rightists. Westerners have tried to label the groupings with a variety of terms: radicals versus conservatives, extremists versus moderates, hard liners versus soft liners, ideologues versus pragmatists. The Chinese Communists now generally describe the divi-

sion as being between persons loyal to the thought of
Mao Tse-tung and those subverted by revisionist, right-
ist, and bourgeois influences. None of these dichoto-
mies accurately describes the complex issues involved,
but they do highlight the fact that under the façade
of unity, policy differences have steadily grown.

While these various trends have been under way,
Mao's role of personal leadership has appeared to
weaken. From the time of the failure of the Great
Leap until 1966, in fact, he seemed to have with-
drawn from day-to-day affairs. He spent much of his
time away from the capital; his public appearances
were rare; and he made fewer and fewer important
public pronouncements.

In 1966 he has again emerged onto the center of
the stage to lead, perhaps for the last time, a renewed
struggle to "revolutionize" Chinese society. It is by no
means wholly clear, however, to what extent recent
events have been directed by Mao himself, or by others
who are using his name. And in any case, the evidence
indicates that the struggle to succeed Mao has already
begun, even if he is still trying to shape and control
its outcome.

1966 has seen the greatest and in many respects most
significant political turbulence within China since the
Communist take over in 1949. Several different developments have converged, of which three are most important. First, there has been an intensification of the
campaign to indoctrinate the entire population in Mao-

ism, to combat revisionism, to shake up the ruling bureaucracy, and to activate China's youth, in order to ensure, as the dominant leaders put it, "continuation of the revolution to the end." Second, there has been mounting debate on many basic issues of national policy. And third, there has been, and continues to be, a major struggle for power. All three of these developments are interconnected, and they all, in a sense, are responses to the anticipated demise of Mao.

The indoctrination campaign, which I discussed earlier, has been growing in scope and intensity ever since the Tenth Party Plenum in 1962. Moreover, one could outline a series of major steps and events from 1963 onward, each of which has raised the campaign to a new level: the glorification of Lei feng as a model cadre, the spread of a nationwide "socialist education" program, the attacks on leading Party and non-Party intellectuals, including Yang Hsien-chen and many other prominent figures, and so on. This year the effort has reached a new peak in the so-called "great proletarian cultural revolution" and Red Guards' campaign. The basic aim has been to try to elevate the thought of Mao Tse-tung to the status of unchallengeable dogma, to suppress all revisionist or bourgeois ideas, to fight against both the drag of Chinese tradition and the subversion of foreign ideas, and to attack all signs of bureaucratism, in order to prepare for the post-Mao period.

The fact that there has been mounting debate on

policy has been made clear in many of the public attacks leveled during the purge this year against those accused of promoting an "anti-Party, anti-socialist, Right Opportunist . . . revisionist line."

To illustrate, let me quote a few of the accusations made in an article entitled "On Three Family Village," published on May 10 in two leading Shanghai papers, *Liberation Daily* (*Chieh Fang Jih Pao*) and *Wen Hui Pao*.[4] This article specifically attacked three men—Wu Han, Vice-Mayor of Peking, Teng T'o, director and former chief editor of the *Peking People's Daily* and a secretary of the Municipal Party Committee of Peking, and Liao Mo-sha, former head of the United Front Department of that Committee. In reality, however, it constituted a much more general attack on all opponents of the current Party line.

In most extravagant language, the authors of the article attacked the "monsters," "freaks," and "poisonous snakes" making up the so-called "anti-Party group." It accused them of mounting "a deliberate, planned and organized attack on the Party and socialism," and of "grossly slandering the Central Committee of the Party and Chairman Mao." More specifically, they were accused of directing their attacks "precisely against the Lushan meeting and against the Central Committee headed by Comrade Mao Tse-tung, with a view to reversing the decisions of that meeting" and of giving "all out support for the attacks of the Right op-

[4] English text in *Peking Review*, No. 1966-22, May 27, 1966.

portunists who had been 'dismissed from office'"; the "Lushan meeting," of course, was the Eighth Party Plenum in 1959 which purged P'eng Teh-huai and clamped down on all so-called "Rightists."

What, exactly, were the men who were the targets of these attacks ostensibly guilty of supporting? They were accused of demanding that the Party "open the door to those 'miscellaneous scholars' who had taken the capitalist road and allow them to lead in 'all kinds of work of leadership' and in 'scientific work'—in other words, in the academic and ideological fields—so as to prepare public opinion for the restoration of capitalism." They were said to have defended the regime's "careerists" and to have urged the Party to "replace the class line by the so-called principle of 'employing people according to their talents' and thereby to train large numbers of successors of the landlords and bourgeoisie 'in a planned way.'" They were linked to those demanding "bourgeois liberalization" who have pressed for expansion of small-scale individual economic enterprises, extension of rural free markets and private plots, and even a return to using individual households as the basis for fixing output quotas. They were charged with favoring a "relaxed mood" and "peaceful evolution," instead of continued class struggle, their "real aim being to subvert the entire system of dictatorship of the proletariat and bring about the restoration of capitalism." Moreover, they were said to "ridicule our Party's policy of self-reliance," to have advocated

" 'uniting with' countries 'stronger than our own' "—meaning the Soviet Union—and to have urged "open collaboration with the reactionaries, both in China and abroad, and the modern revisionists."[5]

The peak of this subversive activity, so the article said, was between 1959 and 1962, when opponents of the current Party line allegedly "took advantage of the three consecutive years of serious natural calamities," to push their cause. But then when Mao at the Tenth Plenum "issued the great call to the whole Party and people throughout the country never to forget class struggle," they "trembled with fright" and beat a retreat. Nevertheless, they kept up dangerous subversive activities; as a result, "the tentacles of the Three Family Village clique have reached into many departments," and they have attracted "admirers and followers in journalistic, educational, literary and art, and academic circles."

Such people must be totally defeated, the article proclaimed. "All those who oppose Mao Tse-tung's thought, obstruct the advance of the socialist revolution, or are hostile to the interests of the revolutionary people of China and the world should be exposed, criticized and knocked down . . . no matter how

[5] Charges of this sort were not new. In December 1964, Chou En-lai at a National People's Congress session attacked those who advocated "liberalization" and hoped for "three freedoms" at home (expansion of private plots, free markets, and individual enterprises) or called for "three reconciliations" abroad (reconciliation with imperialism, the reactionaries, and the revisionists).

famous they are, what influential positions they hold, by whom they are directed or supported, or how numerous their flatterers are. On questions of principle, it is either the East wind or the West wind which must prevail."

This article appeared in early May as the Party purge was moving into high gear, and it revealed that basic ideological and policy questions of the sort that I discussed in earlier chapters are clearly at issue in China today. To date, however, it is difficult to explain the results of the current purge in terms of such issues. In fact, some of the purge's most prominent victims are men who only a short while ago would have been classified as leading hardliners, leftists, and supporters of Maoist principles. This fact suggests that the main struggle so far may have been essentially a contest for power, the start of the succession struggle. Many of the victims of the purge—including many of the lesser ones—may well have supported moderate policies, in opposition to Mao's prescriptions for radicalization, but it seems likely that many others have been ousted mainly because they were believed to pose an actual or potential power threat to the present top leaders and Party line.

The exact origins of the purge are still obscure, and may remain so, but certain facts are known. Apparently there was an important meeting of Central Committee members in September 1965, at which a major reassessment of national policies was undertaken. The purge unfolded subsequent to that meeting. Lin Piao emerged in September as a special apostle of Mao, when he published his famous article on "people's war," and Mao himself disappeared from view in late November, not to reappear until May this year when the first major results of the purge began to be revealed.

In November the Shanghai Party press began to attack Wu Han and others associated with P'eng Chen's municipal Party apparatus in Peking. P'eng's last public appearance was in March.

In April 1966, Kuo Mo-jo, Chairman of both the Chinese Academy of Sciences and the All-China Federation of Literary and Art Circles—who at 74 is the most prominent leader of intellectual and scientific life in China—publicly humbled himself by confessing that he had failed to apply Maoism adequately and declared that "all the works I have written should be burned."[6]

Then, from early May through July, with the army's *Liberation Daily* taking the lead, the propaganda attacks mounted and the purge burst into the open. The first prominent victims were the trio already mentioned, Wu Han, Teng T'o, and Liao Mo-shan, and three periodicals under the Party's Peking Committee, the *Peking Daily* (*Pei Ching Jih Pao*), *Peking Evening*

[6] There are different dates for Kuo's birth, including 1891, 1892, and 1895; 1892 appears to be the correct one. (Despite his "confession" in April 1966, he still appears to be active on the Chinese scene.)

News (*Pei Ching Wan Pao*), and *Frontline* (*Ch'ien Hsien*). The army paper thundered against those who are "responding to the great international anti-Chinese chorus of imperialists, modern revisionists and various reactionaries to revive the Chinese reactionary class," and it attacked "scholars, specialists and professors who oppose the Party and socialism." Wu, said *Red Flag* (*Hung Ch'i*), the Party's main theoretical journal, is "willing to be the slave of the United States and is guilty of scheming and planning for the reactionary Kuomintang clique."

It soon became clear that these attacks were really aimed at men in much higher positions, in the Peking Party apparatus, in the Party's propaganda machine dealing with the press, cultural affairs, and education, and in the military itself as well as in the Public Security apparatus.

In June and July the principal victims—at least to date—were announced. The most important was P'eng Chen, Mayor and Party First Secretary of Peking, ninth-ranking member of the Politburo (only the seven members of the Standing Committee plus Party elder Tung Pi-wu outranked him), and second-ranking member (under Teng Hsiao-p'ing) in the Secretariat. P'eng had long been regarded as a possible contender for succession to Mao. It was announced that he had been removed from his key Peking Party post and replaced by Li Hsueh-feng.

The second major victim was Lu Ting-yi, alternate

member of the Politburo, head of the Central Committee's Propaganda Department and Minister of Culture, the Party's top man in the fields of propaganda, culture, and education ever since 1949. Lu was replaced by T'ao Chu in his Party Department post and by an army officer, Hsiao Wang-tung, in his Ministerial job, while his principal deputy in the Propaganda Department, Ch'en Po-ta (also an alternate Politburo member and editor of *Red Flag*) was identified as the "leader of the group in charge of the cultural revolution under the Party's Central Committee." Also victimized along with Lu was Chou Yang, another Deputy Director of the Propaganda Department, the virtual czar of literature and the arts in China, who had long been resented by Chinese intellectuals as a hardliner.

The third major victim was Lo Jui-ch'ing, member of the Party Secretariat, Minister of Public Security for a decade, and Army Chief of Staff since 1959. Lo was temporarily replaced by one of his deputies, a man named Yang Ch'eng-wu.

With such major figures as its principal targets, the purge, not surprisingly, has subsequently affected thousands of others throughout the country. Especially hard hit to date have been those in propaganda, education, and the cultural fields—persons such as university administrators and teachers, heads of Party Propaganda Departments, newspaper editors, and the like.

In early August, the Party Central Committee held its Eleventh Plenum—the first such meeting for four years—to confirm the shifts in power. The Committee called for intensification of the cultural revolution, and immediately thereafter the Red Guards appeared on the scene.

Clearly, the purge this year has already resulted in the greatest shakeup in the Chinese Communist Party since Mao rose to power, greater even than that involved in the Kao-Jao purge. And the turmoil is not yet over. In fact, the events of 1966 may well prove to be simply the first phase of a succession struggle that could be long and complicated.

From the fragmentary data available, how can one best explain who has been involved in the struggle so far, and what its results have been to date? The most plausible explanation—or at least hypothesis—is that a grouping of opposition elements began to take shape within the Party Politburo and Secretariat, challenging the power of the currently dominant leaders, but Mao, Lin, and their supporters acted decisively to suppress them. Since the challengers included one of the Party's top organization men (who ranked second in the Secretariat), its top propagandist, and its top ex-policeman (who had a powerful position in the army)—these three men occupied two Politburo and three Secretariat seats—the challenge clearly posed a major threat to those at the top and the struggle has obviously been a painful one.

In striking back, Mao relied heavily on the army, the Shanghai Party Committee, the new special group established under the Central Committee to lead the cultural revolution, and the mobilized youth of the country. But apparently he was also able to obtain the support of a coalition of top Politburo leaders, including not only Lin Piao but also other key men such as Chou En-lai, a coalition which included the members of the Politburo's standing Committee who currently hold the greatest power not only in the military establishment, but also in the government bureaucracy. When Mao reappeared in May, after almost six months' absence from public view, these men were ostentatiously photographed with him, along with Teng Hsiao-p'ing. But in the course of the power struggle, many shifts have taken place in power relations within the Politburo, and before the struggle is over more may occur. Whether Lin will collaborate effectively with such men over the long run remains to be seen.

What do these developments portend for the succession, once Mao dies? Until very recently, all evidence pointed to the fact that Mao for years had been consciously grooming Liu Shao-ch'i as his successor. As early as 1945 Liu emerged as second-ranking Party leader, and when he became Chairman of the government in 1959, there was little doubt that he had been designated as Mao's heir. However, the 68-year-old Liu has obviously been downgraded as a result of the current purge, and his future, and Teng's as well, appears to be in doubt. The designated heir now is unquestionably Lin Piao, who at 59 is the youngest member of the Politburo and as leader of the Army has a specially strong power base. In short, if Mao were to die tomorrow, undoubtedly Lin Piao rather than Liu Shao-ch'i would become Mao's successor in a formal sense. It is doubtful, however, that he could consolidate and hold this position successfully without the collaboration or at least acquiescence of the Party machine, and he could not rule the country successfully without the cooperation of the government bureaucracy. He will doubtless have to obtain, therefore, the cooperation of key men whose main roots are in the Party apparatus and government administration, although some present leaders will doubtless be purged.

It should be emphasized, though, that no one outside of Peking's inner circle can really know what present power relationships exist at the center of power in China, and furthermore the present situation could change, suddenly and rapidly.

Perhaps the most important thing to note is that in a basic sense no one can really replace Mao. After Mao dies, therefore, the competition of varied forces within the regime is likely to intensify, and as a consequence there will almost certainly be a greater fluidity of both leadership and policies than in the past.

Some people have observed that the immediate successors to Mao are likely to be men whose backgrounds are similar to his, and that it may take five or ten years or even longer before younger men with different

backgrounds and outlooks—the real second generation
—totally replace the present Party elders. In a sense
this is undoubtedly true.

Nevertheless, the structure of leadership in China has
already been shaken and is certain to undergo very
significant changes during the next few years. The
result of Mao's passing is likely to mean, therefore, less
cohesiveness at the top and greatly increased competition between various policy alternatives and conflicting
group interests, long before the entire first generation
of leaders passes from the scene.

I will not try to recapitulate the various issues and
problems that will be involved in future debates and
conflicts of interest in China, except to reiterate that
although differences on many specific policies will be
involved, over the long run the central competition
will be, as I tried to indicate earlier, between the radicals, extremists, hardliners, leftists, and ideologues, on
the one hand, and the conservatives, moderates, soft-
liners, rightists, and pragmatists, on the other—or, as
Mao himself sees it, between those who are loyal to
the Thought of Mao Tse-tung and are willing to carry
out his prescriptions for the future and those who in
Mao's view are "revisionist" because they favor adap-
tation and change.

What the outcome will be, especially in the short
run, is impossible to predict. The specialists in power,
politics, and ideology—who tend to be hardliners—
will doubtless control the regime's instruments of

power. They may well try to continue pursuing Maoist goals, and attempt to implement radical policies by increasingly coercive methods. But lacking Mao's charismatic qualities, and his ability to preserve unity in the leadership, if they continue to be guided by Mao's Yenan-inspired dogmas, they are likely to be even less successful than he has been in recent years. It is very possible, therefore, that over a period of time Peking's leaders—whoever they are—will be forced increasingly to respond to changing conditions and to pressures exerted by those men within the leadership who advocate more pragmatic and moderate policies. As a new generation of leaders continues to emerge, and to assert itself, the pressures toward some sort of revisionism seem likely to become progressively stronger.

What are the possible implications of all of his for the future policies of the United States and other Western powers?

First of all, we must recognize that change in China's leadership and policies is possible, and while the direction of change in the immediate future is not predictable, it is at least conceivable that future leaders in Peking may consider alternatives quite different from their present radical and militant policies. Mao and those who share his views like to think that they are uniquely capable of manipulating social forces, but it should be amply clear by now that they, like others, are subject to influences and forces beyond their control. It is equally clear, as I have emphasized, that in the years ahead Mao's policies will not be unchallenged in China, for there will be increasingly active competition for leadership, and increasingly intense debate over policy.

In the future competition of forces and influences affecting Chinese policies, domestic factors are likely to be crucial. Probably external influences, exerted by the United States or any other nation, can at most have only a marginal effect on the outcome. But it should not be assumed that they cannot have any effect at all.

Obviously, it would be to our advantage if pragmatists and moderates in China could exert a growing influence on policy. There are not likely to be obvious ways, however, in which we can directly manipulate forces or leaders in China to make this come about. In fact, efforts to do so might well boomerang and be self-defeating. What we can do, however, is adopt policies which indicate to Peking's leaders that they do have a variety of policy options and that we will respond positively to any signs of reasonableness and moderation on their part.

Our aim should be, through a flexible, sophisticated use of varied policies, to demonstrate on the one hand that dogmatic, violent, extreme policies of the sort now advocated by Mao and China's radicals can only be counterproductive, in terms of China's own interests, but at the same time to try to convince Peking's leaders that if China were to pursue more pragmatic and moderate policies, both at home and abroad, it would have a greater chance than at present of achieving some of China's most basic and legitimate goals.

There is certainly no guarantee, whatever we do, that Communist China will inevitably move in the immediate future toward more reasonable policies. But moves in this direction are at least possible, and we, on our part, should do whatever we can to try to convince the leadership in China that this is the course they should pursue.

PART II

Selected Documents

To UNDERSTAND the forces at work in Communist China, now and in the years immediately ahead, it is essential to know Mao Tse-tung's own analysis of these forces and his prescriptions for policies which the Chinese Communist Party should adopt to cope with them. The relevant literature emanating from Peking is enormous, but as indicated in the text of this volume, certain documents are particularly revealing of Mao's diagnosis of the situation and his vision of the future. Among them are the joint *Red Flag-People's Daily* editorial entitled, "On Khrushchov's Phoney Communism and Its Historical Lessons for the World," an English translation of which was published as a pamphlet by the Foreign Language Press, Peking, 1964, and Lin Piao's article, "Long Live the Victory of People's War," an English translation of which was published in *Peking Review* on September 3, 1965. Although portions of these documents have been quoted or summarized in the substantive portion of this volume, their full texts are included here for readers who wish to study them in detail and obtain the full flavor of Mao's argumentation.

Included also are the full texts of two other important documents which state the official position of the currently dominant leaders of the Chinese Communist Party regarding the present struggle in China. These are the "Decision of the Chinese Communist

Party Central Committee Concerning the Great Cultural Revolution" (adopted August 8, 1966), and the "Communiqué of the Eleventh Plenary Session of the Eighth Central Committee of the Communist Party of China" (adopted on August 12, 1966). These two documents, issued by the Chinese Communist Party Central Committee at the time of their Eleventh Plenum in August 1966, were put out by the New China News Agency on August 8 and August 13, respectively, and are published in the August 16 and August 17 issues of Survey of the China Mainland Press, a translation series put out by the American Consulate-General, Hong Kong.

Russian proper names are spelled here as they appear in the Chinese English-language edition, hence "Khrushchov," not "Khrushchev."

DOCUMENT 1

On Khrushchov's Phoney Communism and Its Historical Lessons for the World

—COMMENT ON THE OPEN LETTER OF
THE CENTRAL COMMITTEE OF THE CPSU (IX)

by the Editorial Departments of *Jen Min Jih Pao*
(*People's Daily*) and *Hung Ch'i* (*Red Flag*)

July 14, 1964

FOREIGN LANGUAGES PRESS
PEKING 1964

THE THEORIES of the proletarian revolution and the dictatorship of the proletariat are the quintessence of Marxism-Leninism. The questions of whether revolution should be upheld or opposed and whether the dictatorship of the proletariat should be upheld or opposed have always been the focus of struggle between Marxism-Leninism and all brands of revisionism and are now the focus of struggle between Marxist-Leninists the world over and the revisionist Khrushchov clique.

At the 22nd Congress of the CPSU, the revisionist Khrushchov clique developed their revisionism into a complete system not only by rounding off their anti-revolutionary theories of "peaceful coexistence," "peaceful competition" and "peaceful transition" but also by declaring that the dictatorship of the proletariat is no longer necessary in the Soviet Union and advancing the absurd theories of the "state of the whole people" and the "party of the entire people."

The Programme put forward by the revisionist Khrushchov clique at the 22nd Congress of the CPSU is a programme of phoney communism, a revisionist programme against proletarian revolution and for the abolition of the dictatorship of the proletariat and the proletarian party.

The revisionist Khrushchov clique abolish the dictatorship of the proletariat behind the camouflage of the "state of the whole people," change the proletarian character of the Communist Party of the Soviet Union behind the camouflage of the "party of the entire people" and pave the way for the restoration of capitalism behind that of "full-scale communist construction."

In its Proposal Concerning the General Line of the International Communist Movement dated June 14, 1963, the Central Committee of the Communist Party of China pointed out that it is most absurd in theory and extremely harmful in practice to substitute the "state of the whole people" for the state of the dictatorship of the proletariat and the "party of the entire people" for the vanguard party of the proletariat. This substitution is a great historical retrogression which makes any transition to communism impossible and helps only to restore capitalism.

The Open Letter of the Central Committee of the CPSU and the press of the Soviet Union resort to sophistry in self-justification and charge that our criticisms of the "state of the whole people" and the "party of the entire people" are allegations "far removed from Marxism," betray "isolation from the life of the Soviet people" and are a demand that they "return to the past."

1. On Khrushchov's Phoney Communism

Well, let us ascertain who is actually far removed from Marxism-Leninism, what Soviet life is actually like and who actually wants the Soviet Union to return to the past.

SOCIALIST SOCIETY AND THE DICTATORSHIP
OF THE PROLETARIAT

What is the correct conception of socialist society? Do classes and class struggle exist throughout the stage of socialism? Should the dictatorship of the proletariat be maintained and the socialist revolution be carried through to the end? Or should the dictatorship of the proletariat be abolished so as to pave the way for capitalist restoration? These questions must be answered correctly according to the basic theory of Marxism-Leninism and the historical experience of the dictatorship of the proletariat.

The replacement of capitalist society by socialist society is a great leap in the historical development of human society. Socialist society covers the important historical period of transition from class to classless society. It is by going through socialist society that mankind will enter communist society.

The socialist system is incomparably superior to the capitalist system. In socialist society, the dictatorship of the proletariat replaces bourgeois dictatorship and the public ownership of the means of production replaces private ownership. The proletariat, from being an oppressed and exploited class, turns into the ruling class and a fundamental change takes place in the social position of the working people. Exercising dictatorship over a few exploiters only, the state of the dictatorship of the proletariat practises the broadest democracy among the masses of the working people, a democracy which is impossible in capitalist society. The nationalization of industry and

1. On Khrushchov's Phoney Communism

collectivization of agriculture open wide vistas for the vigorous development of the social productive forces, ensuring a rate of growth incomparably greater than that in any older society.

However, one cannot but see that socialist society is a society born out of capitalist society and is only the first phase of communist society. It is not yet a fully mature communist society in the economic and other fields. It is inevitably stamped with the birth marks of capitalist society. When defining socialist society Marx said:

> What we have to deal with here is a communist society, not as it has *developed* on its own foundations, but, on the contrary, just as it *emerges* from capitalist society; which is thus in every respect, economically, morally and intellectually, still stamped with the birth marks of the old society from whose womb it emerges.[1]

Lenin also pointed out that in socialist society, which is the first phase of communism, "Communism *cannot* as yet be fully ripe economically and entirely free from traditions or traces of capitalism."[2]

In socialist society, the differences between workers and peasants, between town and country, and between manual and mental laborers still remain, bourgeois rights are not yet completely abolished, it is not possible "at once to eliminate the other injustice, which consists in the distribution of articles of consumption 'according to the amount of labor performed' (and not according to

[1] Marx, "Critique of the Gotha Programme," *Selected Works of Marx and Engels*, Foreign Languages Publishing House, Moscow, 1958, Vol. 2, p. 23.

[2] Lenin, "The State and Revolution," *Selected Works*, FLPH, Moscow, 1952, Vol. 2, Part 1, p. 302.

needs),"[3] and therefore differences in wealth still exist. The disappearance of these differences, phenomena and bourgeois rights can only be gradual and long drawn-out. As Marx said, only after these differences have vanished and bourgeois rights have completely disappeared, will it be possible to realize full communism with its principle, "from each according to his ability, to each according to his needs."

Marxism-Leninism and the practice of the Soviet Union, China and other socialist countries all teach us that socialist society covers a very, very long historical stage. Throughout this stage, the class struggle between the bourgeoisie and the proletariat goes on and the question of "who will win" between the roads of capitalism and socialism remains, as does the danger of the restoration of capitalism.

In its Proposal Concerning the General Line of the International Communist Movement dated June 14, 1963, the Central Committee of the Chinese Communist Party states:

> For a very long historical period after the proletariat takes power, class struggle continues as an objective law independent of man's will, differing only in form from what it was before the taking of power.
>
> After the October Revolution, Lenin pointed out a number of times that:
> a) The overthrown exploiters always try in a thousand and one ways to recover the "paradise" they have been deprived of.
> b) New elements of capitalism are constantly and spontaneously generated in the petty-bourgeois atmosphere.

[3] *Ibid.*, p. 296.

c) Political degenerates and new bourgeois elements may emerge in the ranks of the working class and among government functionaries as a result of bourgeois influence and the pervasive, corrupting atmosphere of the petty bourgeoisie.

d) The external conditions for the continuance of class struggle within a socialist country are encirclement by international capitalism, the imperialists' threat of armed intervention and their subversive activities to accomplish peaceful disintegration.

Life has confirmed these conclusions of Lenin's.

In socialist society, the overthrown bourgeoisie and other reactionary classes remain strong for quite a long time, and indeed in certain respects are quite powerful. They have a thousand and one links with the international bourgeoisie. They are not reconciled to their defeat and stubbornly continue to engage in trials of strength with the proletariat. They conduct open and hidden struggles against the proletariat in every field. Constantly parading such signboards as support for socialism, the Soviet system, the Communist Party and Marxism-Leninism, they work to undermine socialism and restore capitalism. Politically, they persist for a long time as a force antagonistic to the proletariat and constantly attempt to overthrow the dictatorship of the proletariat. They sneak into the government organs, public organizations, economic departments and cultural and educational institutions so as to resist or usurp the leadership of the proletariat. Economically, they employ every means to damage socialist ownership by the whole people and socialist collective ownership and to develop the forces of capitalism. In the ideological, cultural and educational fields, they counterpose the bourgeois world outlook to the proletarian world outlook and try to corrupt the proletariat and other working people with bourgeois ideology.

The collectivization of agriculture turns individual into collective farmers and provides favorable conditions for the thorough remoulding of the peasants. However, until collective ownership advances to ownership by the whole people and until the remnants of private economy disappear completely, the peasants inevitably retain some of the inherent characteristics of small producers. In these circumstances spontaneous capitalist tendencies are inevitable, the soil for the growth of new rich peasants still exists and polarization among the peasants may still occur.

The activities of the bourgeoisie as described above, its corrupting effects in the political, economic, ideological and cultural and educational fields, the existence of spontaneous capitalist tendencies among urban and rural small producers, and the influence of the remaining bourgeois rights and the force of habit of the old society all constantly breed political degenerates in the ranks of the working class and Party and government organizations, new bourgeois elements and embezzlers and grafters in state enterprises owned by the whole people and new bourgeois intellectuals in the cultural and educational institutions and intellectual circles. These new bourgeois elements and these political degenerates attack socialism in collusion with the old bourgeois elements and elements of other exploiting classes which have been overthrown but not eradicated. The political degenerates entrenched in the leading organs are particularly dangerous, for they support and shield the bourgeois elements in organs at lower levels.

As long as imperialism exists, the proletariat in the socialist countries will have to struggle both against the bourgeoisie at home and against international imperialism. Imperialism will seize every opportunity and try to undertake armed intervention against the socialist countries or to bring about their peaceful disintegration. It will do its utmost to destroy the socialist countries or to make them degenerate into capitalist countries. The international class struggle will inevitably find its reflection within the socialist countries.

Lenin said:

The transition from capitalism to Communism represents an entire historical epoch. Until this epoch has terminated, the exploiters inevitably cherish the hope of restoration, and this *hope* is converted into *attempts* at restoration.[4]

He also pointed out:

The abolition of classes requires a long, difficult and stubborn *class struggle*, which *after* the overthrow of the power of capital, *after* the destruction of the bourgeois state, *after* the establishment of the dictatorship of the proletariat, *does not disappear* (as the vulgar representatives of the old Socialism and the old Social-Democracy imagine), but merely changes its forms and in many respects becomes more fierce.[5]

Throughout the stage of socialism the class struggle between the proletariat and the bourgeoisie in the political, economic, ideological and cultural and educational fields cannot be stopped. It is a protracted, repeated, tortuous

[4] Lenin, "The Proletarian Revolution and the Renegade Kautsky," *Selected Works*, FLPH, Moscow, Vol. 2, Part 2, p. 61.

[5] Lenin, "Greetings to the Hungarian Workers," *Selected Works*, FLPH, Moscow, Vol. 2, Part 2, pp. 210-11.

and complex struggle. Like the waves of the sea it sometimes rises high and sometimes subsides, is now fairly calm and now very turbulent. It is a struggle that decides the fate of a socialist society. Whether a socialist society will advance to communism or revert to capitalism depends upon the outcome of this protracted struggle.

The class struggle in socialist society is inevitably reflected in the Communist Party. The bourgeoisie and international imperialism both understand that in order to make a socialist country degenerate into a capitalist country, it is first necessary to make the Communist Party degenerate into a revisionist party. The old and new bourgeois elements, the old and new rich peasants and the degenerate elements of all sorts constitute the social basis of revisionism, and they use every possible means to find agents within the Communist Party. The existence of bourgeois influence is the internal source of revisionism and surrender to imperialist pressure the external source. Throughout the stage of socialism, there is inevitable struggle between Marxism-Leninism and various kinds of opportunism—mainly revisionism—in the Communist Parties of socialist countries. The characteristic of this revisionism is that, denying the existence of classes and class struggle, it sides with the bourgeoisie in attacking the proletariat and turns the dictatorship of the proletariat into the dictatorship of the bourgeoisie.

In the light of the experience of the international working-class movement and in accordance with the objective law of class struggle, the founders of Marxism pointed out that the transition from capitalism to communism, from class to classless society, must depend on the dictatorship of the proletariat and that there is no other road.

1. On Khrushchov's Phoney Communism

Marx said that "the class struggle necessarily leads to the *dictatorship of the proletariat*."[6] He also said:

> Between capitalist and communist society lies the period of the revolutionary transformation of the one into the other. There corresponds to this also a political transition period in which the state can be nothing but *the revolutionary dictatorship of the proletariat*.[7]

The development of socialist society is a process of uninterrupted revolution. In explaining revolutionary socialism Marx said:

> This socialism is the *declaration of the permanence of the revolution*, the *class dictatorship* of the proletariat as the necessary transit point to the *abolition of class distinctions generally*, to the abolition of all the relations of production on which they rest, to the abolition of all the social relations that correspond to these relations of production, to the revolutionizing of all the ideas that result from these social relations.[8]

In his struggle against the opportunism of the Second International, Lenin creatively expounded and developed Marx's theory of the dictatorship of the proletariat. He pointed out:

> The dictatorship of the proletariat is not the end of class struggle but its continuation in new forms. The dictatorship of the proletariat is class struggle waged by a proletariat which has been victorious and has taken

[6] "Marx to J. Weydemeyer, March 5, 1852," *Selected Works of Marx and Engels*, FLPH, Moscow, Vol. 2, p. 452.

[7] Marx, "Critique of the Gotha Programme," *Selected Works of Marx and Engels*, FLPH, Moscow, Vol. 2, pp. 32-33.

[8] Marx, "The Class Struggles in France, 1848 to 1850," *Selected Works of Marx and Engels*, FLPH, Moscow, Vol. 1, p. 223.

political power in its hands against a bourgeoisie that has been defeated but not destroyed, a bourgeoisie that has not vanished, not ceased to offer resistance, but that has intensified its resistance.[9]

He also said:

The dictatorship of the proletariat is a persistent struggle—bloody and bloodless, violent and peaceful, military and economic, educational and administrative —against the forces and traditions of the old society.[10]

In his celebrated work *On the Correct Handling of Contradictions Among the People* and in other works, Comrade Mao Tse-tung, basing himself on the fundamental principles of Marxism-Leninism and the historical experience of the dictatorship of the proletariat, gives a comprehensive and systematic analysis of classes and class struggle in socialist society, and creatively develops the Marxist-Leninist theory of the dictatorship of the proletariat.

Comrade Mao Tse-tung examines the objective laws of socialist society from the viewpoint of materialist dialectics. He points out that the universal law of the unity and struggle of opposites operating both in the natural world and in human society is applicable to socialist society, too. In socialist society, class contradictions still remain and class struggle does not die out after the socialist transformation of the ownership of the means of production. The struggle between the two roads of socialism and capital-

[9] Lenin, "Foreword to the Speech 'On Deception of the People with Slogans of Freedom and Equality,'" *Alliance of the Working Class and the Peasantry*, FLPH, Moscow, 1959, p. 302.

[10] Lenin, "'Left-Wing' Communism, an Infantile Disorder," *Selected Works*, FLPH, Moscow, Vol. 2, Part 2, p. 367.

ism runs through the entire stage of socialism. To ensure the success of socialist construction and to prevent the restoration of capitalism, it is necessary to carry the socialist revolution through to the end on the political, economic, ideological and cultural fronts. The complete victory of socialism cannot be brought about in one or two generations; to resolve this question thoroughly requires five or ten generations or even longer.

Comrade Mao Tse-tung stresses the fact that two types of social contradictions exist in socialist society, namely, contradictions among the people and contradictions between ourselves and the enemy, and that the former are very numerous. Only by distinguishing between the two types of contradictions, which are different in nature, and by adopting different measures to handle them correctly is it possible to unite the people, who constitute more than 90 per cent of the population, defeat their enemies, who constitute only a few per cent, and consolidate the dictatorship of the proletariat.

The dictatorship of the proletariat is the basic guarantee for the consolidation and development of socialism, for the victory of the proletariat over the bourgeoisie and of socialism in the struggle between the two roads.

Only by emancipating all mankind can the proletariat ultimately emancipate itself. The historical task of the dictatorship of the proletariat has two aspects, one internal and the other international. The internal task consists mainly of completely abolishing all the exploiting classes, developing socialist economy to the maximum, enhancing the communist consciousness of the masses, abolishing the differences between ownership by the whole people and collective ownership, between workers and peasants, between town and country and between mental and manual laborers, eliminating any possibility of the re-emergence of classes and the restoration of capitalism and providing conditions for the realization of a communist society with its principle, "from each according to his ability, to each according to his needs." The international task consists mainly of preventing attacks by international imperialism (including armed intervention and disintegration by peaceful means) and of giving support to the world revolution until the people of all countries finally abolish imperialism, capitalism and the system of exploitation. Before the fulfilment of both tasks and before the advent of a full communist society, the dictatorship of the proletariat is absolutely necessary.

Judging from the actual situation today, the tasks of the dictatorship of the proletariat are still far from accomplished in any of the socialist countries. In all socialist countries without exception, there are classes and class struggle, the struggle between the socialist and the capitalist roads, the question of carrying the socialist revolution through to the end and the question of preventing the restoration of capitalism. All the socialist countries will have a very long way to go before the differences between ownership by the whole people and collective ownership between workers and peasants, between town and country and between mental and manual laborers are eliminated, before all classes and class differences are abolished and a communist society with its principle, "from each according to his ability, to each according to his needs," is realized. Therefore, it is necessary for all the socialist countries to uphold the dictatorship of the proletariat.

In these circumstances, the abolition of the dictatorship

1. On Khrushchov's Phoney Communism

of the proletariat by the revisionist Khrushchov clique is nothing but the betrayal of socialism and communism.

ANTAGONISTIC CLASSES AND CLASS STRUGGLE
EXIST IN THE SOVIET UNION

In announcing the abolition of the dictatorship of the proletariat in the Soviet Union, the revisionist Khrushchov clique base themselves mainly on the argument that antagonistic classes have been eliminated and that class struggle no longer exists.

But what is the actual situation in the Soviet Union? Are there really no antagonistic classes and no class struggle there?

Following the victory of the Great October Socialist Revolution, the dictatorship of the proletariat was established in the Soviet Union, capitalist private ownership was destroyed and socialist ownership by the whole people and socialist collective ownership were established through the nationalization of industry and the collectivization of agriculture, and great achievements in socialist construction were scored during several decades. All this constituted an indelible victory of tremendous historic significance won by the Communist Party of the Soviet Union and the Soviet people under the leadership of Lenin and Stalin.

However, the old bourgeoisie and other exploiting classes which had been overthrown in the Soviet Union were not eradicated and survived after industry was nationalized and agriculture collectivized. The political and ideological influence of the bourgeoisie remained. Spontaneous capitalist tendencies continued to exist both in the city and in the countryside. New bourgeois elements and kulaks were still incessantly generated. Throughout the long intervening period, the class struggle between the proletariat and the bourgeoisie and the struggle between the socialist and capitalist roads have continued in the political, economic, and ideological spheres.

As the Soviet Union was the first, and at the time the only, country to build socialism and had no foreign experience to go by, and as Stalin departed from Marxist-Leninist dialectics in his understanding of the laws of class struggle in socialist society, he prematurely declared after agriculture was basically collectivized that there were "no longer antagonistic classes"[11] in the Soviet Union and that it was "free of class conflicts,"[12] one-sidedly stressed the internal homogeneity of socialist society and overlooked its contradictions, failed to rely upon the working class and the masses in the struggle against the forces of capitalism and regarded the possibility of the restoration of capitalism as associated only with armed attack by international imperialism. This was wrong both in theory and in practice. Nevertheless, Stalin remained a great Marxist-Leninist. As long as he led the Soviet Party and state, he held fast to the dictatorship of the proletariat and the socialist course, pursued a Marxist-Leninist line and ensured the Soviet Union's victorious advance along the road of socialism.

Ever since Khrushchov seized the leadership of the Soviet Party and state, he has pushed through a whole series of revisionist policies which have greatly hastened the growth of the forces of capitalism and again sharpened

[11] Stalin, "On the Draft Constitution of the U.S.S.R.," *Problems of Leninism*, FLPH, Moscow, 1954, p. 690.

[12] Stalin, "Report to the Eighteenth Congress of the C.P.S.U. (B.) on the Work of the Central Committee," *Problems of Leninism*, FLPH, Moscow, p. 777.

the class struggle between the proletariat and the bourgeoisie and the struggle between the roads of socialism and capitalism in the Soviet Union.

Scanning the reports in Soviet newspapers over the last few years, one finds numerous examples demonstrating not only the presence of many elements of the old exploiting classes in Soviet society, but also the generation of new bourgeois elements on a large scale and the acceleration of class polarization.

Let us first look at the activities of the various bourgeois elements in the Soviet enterprises owned by the whole people.

Leading functionaries of some state-owned factories and their gangs abuse their positions and amass large fortunes by using the equipment and materials of the factories to set up "underground workshops" for private production, selling the products illicitly and dividing the spoils. Here are some examples.

In a Leningrad plant producing military items, the leading functionaries placed their own men in "all key posts" and "turned the state enterprise into a private one." They illicitly engaged in the production of non-military goods and from the sale of fountain pens alone embezzled 1,200,000 old rubles in three years. Among these people was a man who "was a Nepman . . . in the 1920's" and had been a "lifelong thief."[13]

In a silk-weaving mill in Uzbekistan, the manager ganged up with the chief engineer, the chief accountant, the chief of the supply and marketing section, heads of workshops and others, and they all became "new-born entrepreneurs." They purchased more than ten tons of artificial and pure silk through various illegal channels

[13] *Krasnaya Zvezda*, May 19, 1962.

in order to manufacture goods which "did not pass through the accounts." They employed workers without going through the proper procedures and enforced "a twelve-hour working day."[14]

The manager of a furniture factory in Kharkov set up an "illegal knitwear workshop" and carried on secret operations inside the factory. This man "had several wives, several cars, several houses, 176 neck-ties, about a hundred shirts and dozens of suits." He was also a big gambler at the horse-races.[15]

Such people do not operate all by themselves. They invariably work hand in glove with functionaries in the state departments in charge of supplies and in the commercial and other departments. They have their own men in the police and judicial departments who protect them and act as their agents. Even high-ranking officials in the state organs support and shield them. Here are a few examples.

The chief of the workshops affiliated to a Moscow psychoneurological dispensary and his gang set up an "underground enterprise," and by bribery "obtained fifty-eight knitting machines" and a large amount of raw material. They entered into business relations with "fifty-two factories, handicraft co-operatives and collective farms" and made three million rubles in a few years. They bribed functionaries of the Department for Combating Theft of Socialist Property and Speculation, controllers, inspectors, instructors and others.[16]

The manager of a machinery plant in the Russian Fed-

---

[14] *Pravda Vostoka*, Oct. 8, 1963.

[15] *Pravda Ukrainy*, May 18, 1962.

[16] *Izvestia*, Oct. 20, 1963, and *Izvestia Sunday Supplement*, No. 12, 1964.

eration, together with the deputy manager of a second machinery plant and other functionaries, or forty-three persons in all, stole more than nine hundred looms and sold them to factories in Central Asia, Kazakhstan, the Caucasus and other places, whose leading functionaries used them for illicit production.[17]

In the Kirghiz SSR, a gang of over forty embezzlers and grafters, having gained control of two factories, organized underground production and plundered more than thirty million rubles' worth of state property. This gang included the Chairman of the Planning Commission of the Republic, a Vice-Minister of Commerce, seven bureau chiefs and division chiefs of the Republic's Council of Ministers, National Economic Council and State Control Commission, as well as "a big kulak who had fled from exile."[18]

These examples show that the factories which have fallen into the clutches of such degenerates are socialist enterprises only in name, that in fact they have become capitalist enterprises by which these persons enrich themselves. The relationship of such persons to the workers has turned into one between exploiters and exploited, between oppressors and oppressed. Are not such degenerates who possess and make use of means of production to exploit the labor of others out-and-out bourgeois elements? Are not their accomplices in government organizations, who work hand in glove with them, participate in many types of exploitation, engage in embezzlement, accept bribes, and share the spoils, also out-and-out bourgeois elements?

Obviously all these people belong to a class that is an-

[17] *Komsomolskaya Pravda,* Aug. 9, 1963.
[18] *Sovietskaya Kirghizia,* Jan. 9, 1962.

tagonistic to the proletariat—they belong to the bourgeoisie. Their activities against socialism are definitely class struggle with the bourgeoisie attacking the proletariat.

Now let us look at the activities of various kulak elements on the collective farms.

Some leading collective-farm functionaries and their gangs steal and speculate at will, freely squander public money and fleece the collective farmers. Here are some examples.

The chairman of a collective farm in Uzbekistan "held the whole village in terror." All the important posts on this farm "were occupied by his in-laws and other relatives and friends." He squandered "over 132,000 rubles of the collective farm for his personal 'needs'." He had a car, two motor-cycles and three wives, each with "a house of her own."[19]

The chairman of a collective farm in the Kursk Region regarded the farm as his "hereditary estate." He conspired with its accountant, cashier, chief warehouse-keeper, agronomist, general-store manager and others. Shielding each other, they "fleeced the collective farmers" and pocketed more than a hundred thousand rubles in a few years.[20]

The chairman of a collective farm in the Ukraine made over 50,000 rubles at its expense by forging purchase certificates and cash-account orders in collusion with its woman accountant, who had been praised for keeping "model accounts" and whose deeds had been displayed at the Moscow Exhibition of Achievements of the National Economy.[21]

[19] *Selskaya Zhizn,* June 26, 1962.
[20] *Ekonomicheskaya Gazeta,* No. 35, 1963.
[21] *Selskaya Zhizn,* Aug. 14, 1963.

1. On Khrushchov's Phoney Communism

The chairman of a collective farm in the Alma-Ata Region specialized in commercial speculation. He bought "fruit juice in the Ukraine or Uzbekistan, and sugar and alcohol from Djambul," processed them and then sold the wine at very high prices in many localities. In this farm a winery was created with a capacity of over a million litres a year, its speculative commercial network spread throughout the Kazakhstan SSR, and commercial speculation became one of the farm's main sources of income.[22]

The chairman of a collective farm in Byelorussia considered himself "a feudal princeling on the farm" and acted "personally" in all matters. He lived not on the farm but in the city or in his own splendid villa, and was always busy with "various commercial machinations" and "illegal deals." He bought cattle from the outside, represented them as the products of his collective farm and falsified output figures. And yet "not a few commendatory newspaper reports" had been published about him and he had been called a "model leader."[23]

These examples show that collective farms under the control of such functionaries virtually become their private property. Such men turn socialist collective economic enterprises into economic enterprises of new kulaks. There are often people in their superior organizations who protect them. Their relationship to the collective farmers has likewise become that of oppressors to oppressed, of exploiters to exploited. Are not such neo-exploiters who ride on the backs of the collective farmers one hundred-per-cent neo-kulaks?

Obviously, they all belong to a class that is antagonistic to the proletariat and the laboring farmers, belong to the kulak or rural bourgeois class. Their anti-socialist activities

[22] *Pravda*, Jan. 14, 1962. [23] *Pravda*, Feb. 6, 1961.

are precisely class struggle with the bourgeoisie attacking the proletariat and the laboring farmers.

Apart from the bourgeois elements in state enterprises and collective farms, there are many others in both town and country in the Soviet Union.

Some of them set up private enterprises for private production and sale; others organize contractor teams and openly undertake construction jobs for state or cooperative enterprises; still others open private hotels. A "Soviet woman capitalist" in Leningrad hired workers to make nylon blouses for sale, and her "daily income amounted to 700 new rubles."[24] The owner of a workshop in the Kursk Region made felt boots for sale at speculative prices. He had in his possession 540 pairs of felt boots, eight kilogrammes of gold coins, 3,000 metres of high-grade textiles, 20 carpets, 1,200 kilogrammes of wool and many other valuables.[25] A private entrepreneur in the Gomel Region "hired workers and artisans" and in the course of two years secured contracts for the construction and overhauling of furnaces in twelve factories at a high price.[26] In the Orenburg Region there are "hundreds of private hotels and trans-shipment points," and "the money of the collective farms and the state is continuously streaming into the pockets of the hostelry owners."[27]

Some engage in commercial speculation, making tremendous profits through buying cheap and selling dear or bringing goods from far away. In Moscow there are a great many speculators engaged in the re-sale of agricultural produce. They "bring to Moscow tons of citrus fruit,

[24] *Izvestia*, April 9, 1963.
[25] *Sovietskaya Rossiya*, Oct. 9, 1960.
[26] *Izvestia*, Oct. 18, 1960.
[27] *Selskaya Zhizn*, July 17, 1963.

apples and vegetables and re-sell them at speculative prices." "These profit-grabbers are provided with every facility, with market inns, storerooms and other services at their disposal."[28] In the Krasnodar Territory, a speculator set up her own agency and "employed twelve salesmen and two stevedores." She transported "thousands of hogs, hundreds of quintals of grain and hundreds of tons of fruit" from the rural areas to the Don Basin and moved "great quantities of stolen slag bricks, whole wagons of glass" and other building materials from the city to the villages. She reaped huge profits out of such re-sale.[29]

Others specialize as brokers and middlemen. They have wide contacts and through them one can get anything in return for a bribe. There was a broker in Leningrad who "though he is not the Minister of Trade, controls all the stocks," and "though he holds no post on the railway, disposes of wagons." He could obtain "things the stocks of which are strictly controlled, from outside the stocks." "All the store-houses in Leningrad are at his service." For delivering goods, he received huge "bonuses"—700,000 rubles from one timber combine in 1960 alone. In Leningrad, there is "a whole group" of such brokers.[30]

These private entrepreneurs and speculators are engaged in the most naked capitalist exploitation. Isn't it clear that they belong to the bourgeoisie, the class antagonistic to the proletariat?

Actually the Soviet press itself calls these people "Soviet capitalists," "new-born entrepreneurs," "private entrepreneurs," "newly-emerged kulaks," "speculators," "exploiters," etc. Aren't the revisionist Khrushchov clique

[28] *Ekonomicheskaya Gazeta*, No. 27, 1963.
[29] *Literaturnaya Gazeta*, July 27 and Aug. 17, 1963.
[30] *Sovietskaya Rossiya*, Jan. 27, 1961.

contradicting themselves when they assert that antagonistic classes do not exist in the Soviet Union?

The facts cited above are only a part of those published in the Soviet press. They are enough to shock people, but there are many more which have not been published, many bigger and more serious cases which are covered up and shielded. We have quoted the above data in order to answer the question whether there are antagonistic classes and class struggle in the Soviet Union. These data are readily available and even the revisionist Khrushchov clique are unable to deny them.

These data suffice to show that the unbridled activities of the bourgeoisie against the proletariat are widespread in the Soviet Union, in the city as well as the countryside, in industry as well as agriculture, in the sphere of production as well as the sphere of circulation, all the way from the economic departments to Party and government organizations, and from the grass-roots to the higher leading bodies. These anti-socialist activities are nothing if not the sharp class struggle of the bourgeoisie against the proletariat.

It is not strange that attacks on socialism should be made in a socialist country by old and new bourgeois elements. There is nothing terrifying about this so long as the leadership of the Party and state remains a Marxist-Leninist one. But in the Soviet Union today, the gravity of the situation lies in the fact that the revisionist Khrushchov clique have usurped the leadership of the Soviet Party and state and that a privileged bourgeois stratum has emerged in Soviet society.

We shall deal with this problem in the following section.

1. On Khrushchov's Phoney Communism

THE SOVIET PRIVILEGED STRATUM AND
THE REVISIONIST KHRUSHCHOV CLIQUE

The privileged stratum in contemporary Soviet society is composed of degenerate elements from among the leading cadres of Party and government organizations, enterprises and farms as well as bourgeois intellectuals; it stands in opposition to the workers, the peasants and the overwhelming majority of the intellectuals and cadres of the Soviet Union.

Lenin pointed out soon after the October Revolution that bourgeois and petty-bourgeois ideologies and force of habit were encircling and influencing the proletariat from all directions and were corrupting certain of its sections. This circumstance led to the emergence from among the Soviet officials and functionaries both of bureaucrats alienated from the masses and of new bourgeois elements. Lenin also pointed out that although the high salaries paid to the bourgeois technical specialists staying on to work for the Soviet regime were necessary, they were having a corrupting influence on it.

Therefore, Lenin laid great stress on waging persistent struggles against the influence of bourgeois and petty-bourgeois ideologies, on arousing the broad masses to take part in government work, on ceaselessly exposing and purging bureaucrats and new bourgeois elements in the Soviet organs, and on creating conditions that would bar the existence and reproduction of the bourgeoisie. Lenin pointed out sharply that "without a systematic and determined struggle to improve the apparatus, we shall perish before the basis of socialism is created."[81]

[81] Lenin, "Plan of the Pamphlet 'On the Food Tax,'" *Collected Works*, 4th Russian ed., Moscow, Vol. 32, p. 301.

1. On Khrushchov's Phoney Communism

At the same time, he laid great stress on adherence to the principle of the Paris Commune in wage policy, that is, all public servants were to be paid wages corresponding to those of the workers and only bourgeois specialists were to be paid high salaries. From the October Revolution to the period of Soviet economic rehabilitation, Lenin's directives were in the main observed; the leading personnel of the Party and government organizations and enterprises and Party members among the specialists received salaries roughly equivalent to the wages of workers.

At that time, the Communist Party and the government of the Soviet Union adopted a number of measures in the sphere of politics and ideology and in the system of distribution to prevent leading cadres in any department from abusing their powers or degenerating morally or politically.

The Communist Party of the Soviet Union headed by Stalin adhered to the dictatorship of the proletariat and the road of socialism and waged a staunch struggle against the forces of capitalism. Stalin's struggles against the Trotskyites, Zinovievites and Bukharinites were in essence a reflection within the Party of the class struggle between the proletariat and the bourgeoisie and of the struggle between the two roads of socialism and capitalism. Victory in these struggles smashed the vain plot of the bourgeoisie to restore capitalism in the Soviet Union.

It cannot be denied that before Stalin's death high salaries were already being paid to certain groups and that some cadres had already degenerated and become bourgeois elements. The Central Committee of the CPSU pointed out in its report to the 19th Party Congress in October 1952 that degeneration and corruption had appeared in certain Party organizations. The leaders of

1. On Khrushchov's Phoney Communism

these organizations had turned them into small communities composed exclusively of their own people, "setting their group interests higher than the interests of the Party and the state." Some executives of industrial enterprises "forget that the enterprises entrusted to their charge are state enterprises, and try to turn them into their own private domain." "Instead of safeguarding the common husbandry of the collective farms," some Party and Soviet functionaries and some cadres in agricultural departments "engage in filching collective-farm property." In the cultural, artistic and scientific fields too, works attacking and smearing the socialist system had appeared and a monopolistic "Arakcheyev regime" had emerged among the scientists.

Since Khrushchov usurped the leadership of the Soviet Party and state, there has been a fundamental change in the state of the class struggle in the Soviet Union.

Khrushchov has carried out a series of revisionist policies serving the interests of the bourgeoisie and rapidly swelling the forces of capitalism in the Soviet Union.

On the pretext of "combating the personality cult," Khrushchov has defamed the dictatorship of the proletariat and the socialist system and thus in fact paved the way for the restoration of capitalism in the Soviet Union. In completely negating Stalin, he has in fact negated Marxism-Leninism which was upheld by Stalin and opened the floodgates for the revisionist deluge.

Khrushchov has substituted "material incentive" for the socialist principle, "from each according to his ability, to each according to his work." He has widened, and not narrowed, the gap between the incomes of a small minority and those of the workers, peasants and ordinary intellectuals. He has supported the degenerates in leading

positions, encouraging them to become even more un-
scrupulous in abusing their powers and to appropriate
the fruits of labor of the Soviet people. Thus he has accelerated the polarization of classes in Soviet society.

Khrushchov sabotages the socialist planned economy,
applies the capitalist principle of profit, develops capitalist
free competition and undermines socialist ownership by
the whole people.

Khrushchov attacks the system of socialist agricultural
planning, describing it as "bureaucratic" and "unnecessary." Eager to learn from the big proprietors of American farms, he is encouraging capitalist management,
fostering a kulak economy and undermining the socialist
collective economy.

Khrushchov is peddling bourgeois ideology, bourgeois
liberty, equality, fraternity and humanity, inculcating
bourgeois idealism and metaphysics and the reactionary
ideas of bourgeois individualism, humanism and pacifism among the Soviet people, and debasing socialist
morality. The rotten bourgeois culture of the West is now
fashionable in the Soviet Union, and socialist culture is
ostracized and attacked.

Under the signboard of "peaceful coexistence," Khrushchov has been colluding with U. S. imperialism, wrecking
the socialist camp and the international communist movement, opposing the revolutionary struggles of the oppressed peoples and nations, practising great-power chauvinism and national egoism and betraying proletarian
internationalism. All this is being done for the protection
of the vested interests of a handful of people, which he
places above the fundamental interests of the peoples of
the Soviet Union, the socialist camp and the whole world.

The line Khrushchov pursues is a revisionist line

through and through. Guided by this line, not only have the old bourgeois elements run wild but new bourgeois elements have appeared in large numbers among the leading cadres of the Soviet Party and government, the chiefs of state enterprises and collective farms, and the higher intellectuals in the fields of culture, art, science and technology.

In the Soviet Union at present, not only have the new bourgeois elements increased in number as never before, but their social status has fundamentally changed. Before Khrushchov came to power, they did not occupy the ruling position in Soviet society. Their activities were restricted in many ways and they were subject to attack. But since Khrushchov took over, usurping the leadership of the Party and the state step by step, the new bourgeois elements have gradually risen to the ruling position in the Party and government and in the economic, cultural and other departments, and formed a privileged stratum in Soviet society.

This privileged stratum is the principal component of the bourgeoisie in the Soviet Union today and the main social basis of the revisionist Khrushchov clique. The revisionist Khrushchov clique are the political representatives of the Soviet bourgeoisie, and particularly of its privileged stratum.

The revisionist Khrushchov clique have carried out one purge after another and replaced one group of cadres after another throughout the country, from the central to the local bodies, from leading Party and government organizations to economic and cultural and educational departments, dismissing those they do not trust and planting their protégés in leading posts.

Take the Central Committee of the CPSU as an example. The statistics show that nearly seventy per cent of the members of the Central Committee of the CPSU who were elected at its 19th Congress in 1952 were purged in the course of the 20th and 22nd Congresses held respectively in 1956 and 1961. And nearly fifty per cent of the members of the Central Committee who were elected at the 20th Congress were purged at the time of the 22nd Congress.

Or take the local organizations. On the eve of the 22nd Congress, on the pretext of "renewing the cadres," the revisionist Khrushchov clique, according to incomplete statistics, removed from office forty-five per cent of the members of the Party Central Committees of the Union Republics and of the Party Committees of the Territories and Regions, and forty per cent of the members of the Municipal and District Party Committees. In 1963, on the pretext of dividing the Party into "industrial" and "agricultural" Party committees, they further replaced more than half the members of the Central Committees of the Union Republics and of the Regional Party Committees.

Through this series of changes the Soviet privileged stratum has gained control of the Party, the government and other important organizations.

The members of this privileged stratum have converted the function of serving the masses into the privilege of dominating them. They are abusing their powers over the means of production and of livelihood for the private benefit of their small clique.

The members of this privileged stratum appropriate the fruits of the Soviet people's labor and pocket incomes that are dozens or even a hundred times those of the average Soviet worker and peasant. They not only secure high incomes in the form of high salaries, high awards, high royalties and a great variety of personal subsidies, but also use their privileged position to appropriate public property by graft and bribery. Completely divorced from the working people of the Soviet Union, they live the parasitical and decadent life of the bourgeoisie.

The members of this privileged stratum have become utterly degenerate ideologically, have completely departed from the revolutionary traditions of the Bolshevik Party and discarded the lofty ideals of the Soviet working class. They are opposed to Marxism-Leninism and socialism. They betray the revolution and forbid others to make revolution. Their sole concern is to consolidate their economic position and political rule. All their activities revolve around the private interests of their own privileged stratum.

Having usurped the leadership of the Soviet Party and state, the Khrushchov clique are turning the Marxist-Leninist Communist Party of the Soviet Union with its glorious revolutionary history into a revisionist party; they are turning the Soviet state under the dictatorship of the proletariat into a state under the dictatorship of the revisionist Khrushchov clique; and, step by step, they are turning socialist ownership by the whole people and socialist collective ownership into ownership by the privileged stratum.

People have seen how in Yugoslavia, although the Tito clique still displays the banner of "socialism," a bureaucrat bourgeoisie opposed to the Yugoslav people has gradually come into being since the Tito clique took the road of revisionism, transforming the Yugoslav state from a dictatorship of the proletariat into the dictatorship of the bureaucrat bourgeoisie and its socialist public economy into state capitalism. Now people see the Khrushchov clique taking the road already travelled by the Tito clique. Khrushchov looks to Belgrade as his Mecca, saying again and again that he will learn from the Tito clique's experience and declaring that he and the Tito clique "belong to one and the same idea and are guided by the same theory."[32] This is not at all surprising.

As a result of Khrushchov's revisionism, the first socialist country in the world built by the great Soviet people with their blood and sweat is now facing an unprecedented danger of capitalist restoration.

The Khrushchov clique are spreading the tale that "there are no longer antagonistic classes and class struggle in the Soviet Union" in order to cover up the facts about their own ruthless class struggle against the Soviet people.

The Soviet privileged stratum represented by the revisionist Khrushchov clique constitutes only a few per cent of the Soviet population. Among the Soviet cadres its numbers are also small. It stands diametrically opposed to the Soviet people, who constitute more than 90 per cent of the total population, and to the great majority of the Soviet cadres and Communists. The contradiction between the Soviet people and this privileged stratum is now the principal contradiction inside the Soviet Union, and it is an irreconcilable and antagonistic class contradiction.

The glorious Communist Party of the Soviet Union, which was built by Lenin, and the great Soviet people displayed epoch-making revolutionary initiative in the October Socialist Revolution, they showed their heroism and stamina in defeating the White Guards and the armed intervention by more than a dozen imperialist countries,

[32] N. S. Khrushchov, Interview with Foreign Correspondents at Brioni in Yugoslavia, Aug. 28, 1963.

they scored unprecedentedly brilliant achievements in the struggle for industrialization and agricultural collectivization, and they won a tremendous victory in the Patriotic War against the German fascists and saved all mankind. Even under the rule of the Khrushchov clique, the mass of the members of the CPSU and the Soviet people are carrying on the glorious revolutionary traditions nurtured by Lenin and Stalin, and they still uphold socialism and aspire to communism.

The broad masses of the Soviet workers, collective farmers and intellectuals are seething with discontent against the oppression and exploitation practised by the privileged stratum. They have come to see ever more clearly the revisionist features of the Khrushchov clique which is betraying socialism and restoring capitalism. Among the ranks of the Soviet cadres, there are many who still persist in the revolutionary stand of the proletariat, adhere to the road of socialism and firmly oppose Khrushchov's revisionism. The broad masses of the Soviet people, of Communists and cadres are using various means to resist and oppose the revisionist line of the Khrushchov clique, so that the revisionist Khrushchov clique cannot so easily bring about the restoration of capitalism. The great Soviet people are fighting to defend the glorious traditions of the Great October Revolution, to preserve the great gains of socialism and to smash the plot for the restoration of capitalism.

REFUTATION OF THE SO-CALLED STATE OF
THE WHOLE PEOPLE

At the 22nd Congress of the CPSU Khrushchov openly raised the banner of opposition to the dictatorship of the proletariat, announcing the replacement of the state of the dictatorship of the proletariat by the "state of the whole people." It is written in the Programme of the CPSU that the dictatorship of the proletariat "has ceased to be indispensable in the U.S.S.R." and that "the state, which arose as a state of the dictatorship of the proletariat, has, in the new, contemporary stage, became a state of the entire people."

Anyone with a little knowledge of Marxism-Leninism knows that the concept of the state is a class concept. Lenin pointed out that "the distinguishing feature of the state is the existence of a separate class of people in whose hands *power* is concentrated."[33] The state is a weapon of class struggle, a machine by means of which one class represses another. Every state is the dictatorship of a definite class. So long as the state exists, it cannot possibly stand above class or belong to the whole people.

The proletariat and its political party have never concealed their views; they say explicitly that the very aim of the proletarian socialist revolution is to overthrow bourgeois rule and establish the dictatorship of the proletariat. After the victory of the socialist revolution, the proletariat and its party must strive unremittingly to fulfill the historical tasks of the dictatorship of the proletariat and eliminate classes and class differences, so that the state will wither away. It is only the bourgeoisie and its parties which in their attempt to hoodwink the masses try by every means to cover up the class nature of state power and describe the state machinery under their control as being "of the whole people" and "above class."

The fact that Khrushchov has announced the abolition

[33] Lenin, "The Economic Content of Narodism and the Criticism of It in Mr. Struve's Book," *Collected Works*, FLPH, Moscow, 1960, Vol. 1, p. 419.

of the dictatorship of the proletariat in the Soviet Union and advanced the thesis of the "state of the whole people" demonstrates that he has replaced the Marxist-Leninist teachings on the state by bourgeois falsehoods.

When Marxist-Leninists criticized their fallacies, the revisionist Khrushchov clique hastily defended themselves and tried hard to invent a so-called theoretical basis for the "state of the whole people." They now assert that the historical period of the dictatorship of the proletariat mentioned by Marx and Lenin refers only to the transition from capitalism to the first stage of communism and not to its higher stage. They further assert that "the dictatorship of the proletariat will cease to be necessary before the state withers away"[34] and that after the end of the dictatorship of the proletariat, there is yet another stage, the "state of the whole people."

These are out-and-out sophistries.

In his *Critique of the Gotha Programme*, Marx advanced the well-known axiom that the dictatorship of the proletariat is the state of the period of transition from capitalism to communism. Lenin gave a clear explanation of this Marxist axiom.

He said:

> In his *Critique of the Gotha Programme* Marx wrote:
> Between capitalist and communist society lies the period of the revolutionary transformation of the one into the other. There corresponds to this also a political transition period in which the state can be nothing but *the revolutionary dictatorship of the proletariat.*

> Up to now this axiom has never been disputed by

[34] *Pravda* editorial board's article, "Programme for the Building of Communism," Aug. 18, 1961.

Socialists, and yet it implies the recognition of the existence of the *state* right up to the time when victorious socialism has grown into complete communism.[35]

Lenin further said:

The essence of Marx's teaching on the state has been mastered only by those who understand that the dictatorship of a *single* class is necessary not only for every class society in general, not only for the *proletariat* which has overthrown the bourgeoisie, but also for the entire *historical period* which separates capitalism from "classless society," from Communism.[36]

It is perfectly clear that according to Marx and Lenin, the historical period throughout which the state of the dictatorship of the proletariat exists, is not merely the period of transition from capitalism to the first stage of communism, as alleged by the revisionist Khrushchov clique, but the entire period of transition from capitalism to "complete communism," to the time when all class differences will have been eliminated and "classless society" realized, that is to say, to the higher stage of communism.

It is equally clear that the state in the transition period referred to by Marx and Lenin is the dictatorship of the proletariat and not anything else. The dictatorship of the proletariat is the form of the state in the entire period of transition from capitalism to the higher stage of communism, and also the last form of the state in human history.

[35] Lenin, "The Discussion on Self-Determination Summed Up," *Collected Works*, International Publishers, New York, 1942, Vol. 19, pp. 269-70.
[36] Lenin, "The State and Revolution," *Selected Works*, FLPH, Moscow, Vol. 2, Part 1, p. 234.

1. On Khrushchov's Phoney Communism

The withering away of the dictatorship of the proletariat will mean the withering away of the state. Lenin said:

> Marx deduced from the whole history of Socialism and of the political struggle that the state was bound to disappear, and that the transitional form of its disappearance (the transition from state to nonstate) would be the "proletariat organized as the ruling class."[37]

Historically the dictatorship of the proletariat may take different forms from one country to another and from one period to another, but in essence it will remain the same. Lenin said:

> The transition from capitalism to Communism certainly cannot but yield a tremendous abundance and variety of political forms, but the essence will inevitably be the same: *the dictatorship of the proletariat.*[38]

It can thus be seen that it is absolutely not the view of Marx and Lenin but an invention of the revisionist Khrushchov that the end of the dictatorship of the proletariat will precede the withering away of the state and will be followed by yet another stage, "the state of the whole people."

In arguing for their anti-Marxist-Leninist views, the revisionist Khrushchov clique have taken great pains to find a sentence from Marx and distorted it by quoting it out of context. They have arbitrarily described the future *nature of the state* [*Staatswesen* in German] of communist society referred to by Marx in his *Critique of the Gotha Programme* as the " 'state of communist society,' which is no longer a dictatorship of the proletariat."[39] They glee-

[37] *Ibid.*, pp. 256-57.   [38] *Ibid.*, p. 234.
[39] M. A. Suslov, Report at the Plenary Meeting of the Central Committee of the CPSU, Feb. 1964. (*New Times*, English ed., No. 15, 1964, p. 62.)

fully announced that the Chinese would not dare to quote this from Marx. Apparently the revisionist Khrushchov clique think it is very helpful to them.

As it happens, Lenin seems to have foreseen that revisionists would make use of this phrase to distort Marxism. In his *Marxism on the State*, Lenin gave an excellent explanation of it. He said, ". . . the dictatorship of the proletariat is a 'political transition period.' . . . But Marx goes on to speak of 'the future *nature of the state* [*Staatswesen* in German] of communist society'!! Thus, there will be a state even in '*communist* society'!! Is there not a contradiction in this?" Lenin answered, "No." He then tabulated the three stages in the process of development from the bourgeois state to the withering away of the state:

The first stage—in capitalist society, the state is needed by the bourgeoisie—the bourgeois state.

The second stage—in the period of transition from capitalism to communism, the state is needed by the proletariat—the state of the dictatorship of the proletariat.

The third stage—in communist society, the state is not necessary, it withers away.

He concluded: "Complete consistency and clarity!!"

In Lenin's tabulation, only the bourgeois state, the state of the dictatorship of the proletariat and the withering away of the state are to be found. By precisely this tabulation Lenin made it clear that when communism is reached the state withers away and becomes non-existent.

Ironically enough, the revisionist Khrushchov clique also quoted this very passage from Lenin's *Marxism on the State* in the course of defending their error. And then they proceeded to make the following idiotic statement:

1. On Khrushchov's Phoney Communism

In our country the first two periods referred to by Lenin in the opinion quoted already belong to history. In the Soviet Union a state of the whole people—*a communist state system*, the state of the *first phase of communism*, has arisen and is developing.[40]

If the first two periods referred to by Lenin have already become a thing of the past in the Soviet Union, then the state should be withering away, and where could a "state of the whole people" come from? If the state is not yet withering away, then it ought to be the dictatorship of the proletariat and under absolutely no circumstances a "state of the whole people."

In arguing for their "state of the whole people," the revisionist Khrushchov clique exert themselves to vilify the dictatorship of the proletariat as undemocratic. They assert that only by replacing the state of the dictatorship of the proletariat by the "state of the whole people" can democracy be further developed and turned into "genuine democracy for the whole people." Khrushchov has pretentiously said that the abolition of the dictatorship of the proletariat exemplifies "a line of energetically developing democracy" and that "proletarian democracy is becoming socialist democracy of the whole people."[41]

These utterances can only show that their authors either are completely ignorant of the Marxist-Leninist teachings on the state or are maliciously distorting them.

Anyone with a little knowledge of Marxism-Leninism

[40] "From the Party of the Working Class to the Party of the Whole Soviet People," editorial board's article of *Partyinaya Zhizn*, Moscow, No. 8, 1964.

[41] N. S. Khrushchov, "Report of the Central Committee of the CPSU," and "On the Programme of the CPSU," delivered at the 22nd Congress of the CPSU, October 1961.

knows that the concept of democracy as a form of the state, like that of dictatorship, is a class one. There can only be class democracy, there cannot be "democracy for the whole people."

Lenin said:

Democracy for the vast majority of the people, and suppression by force, i.e., exclusion from democracy, of the exploiters and oppressors of the people—this is the change democracy undergoes during the *transition* from capitalism to Communism.[42]

Dictatorship over the exploiting classes and democracy among the working people—these are the two aspects of the dictatorship of the proletariat. It is only under the dictatorship of the proletariat that democracy for the masses of the working people can be developed and expanded to an unprecedented extent. Without the dictatorship of the proletariat there can be no genuine democracy for the working people.

Where there is bourgeois democracy there is no proletarian democracy, and where there is proletarian democracy there is no bourgeois democracy. The one excludes the other. This is inevitable and admits of no compromise. The more thoroughly bourgeois democracy is eliminated, the more will proletarian democracy flourish. In the eyes of the bourgeoisie, any country where this occurs is lacking in democracy. But actually this is the promotion of proletarian democracy and the elimination of bourgeois democracy. As proletarian democracy develops, bourgeois democracy is eliminated.

This fundamental Marxist-Leninist thesis is opposed by

[42] Lenin, "The State and Revolution," *Selected Works*, FLPH, Moscow, Vol. 2, Part 1, p. 291.

1. On Khrushchov's Phoney Communism

the revisionist Khrushchov clique. In fact, they hold that so long as enemies are subjected to dictatorship there is no democracy and that the only way to develop democracy is to abolish the dictatorship over enemies, stop suppressing them and institute "democracy for the whole people."

Their view is cast from the same mould as the renegade Kautsky's concept of "pure democracy."

In criticizing Kautsky Lenin said:

> . . . "pure democracy" is not only an *ignorant* phrase, revealing a lack of understanding both of the class struggle and of the nature of the state, but also a thrice-empty phrase, since in communist society democracy will *wither away* in the process of changing and becoming a habit, but will never be "pure" democracy.[43]

He also pointed out:

> The dialectics (course) of the development is as follows: from absolutism to bourgeois democracy; from bourgeois to proletarian democracy; from proletarian democracy to none.[44]

That is to say, in the higher stage of communism proletarian democracy will wither away along with the elimination of classes and the withering away of the dictatorship of the proletariat.

To speak plainly, as with the "state of the whole people," the "democracy for the whole people" proclaimed by Khrushchov is a hoax. In thus retrieving the tattered garments of the bourgeoisie and the old-line revisionists, patching them up and adding a label of his own, Khru-

[43] Lenin, "The Proletarian Revolution and the Renegade Kautsky," *Selected Works*, FLPH, Moscow, Vol. 2, Part 2, p. 48.

[44] Lenin, *Marxism on the State*, Russian ed., Moscow, 1958, p. 42.

shchov's sole purpose is to deceive the Soviet people and the revolutionary people of the world and cover up his betrayal of the dictatorship of the proletariat and his opposition to socialism.

What is the essence of Khrushchov's "state of the whole people"?

Khrushchov has abolished the dictatorship of the proletariat in the Soviet Union and established a dictatorship of the revisionist clique headed by himself, that is, a dictatorship of a privileged stratum of the Soviet bourgeoisie. Actually his "state of the whole people" is not a state of the dictatorship of the proletariat but a state in which his small revisionist clique wield their dictatorship over the masses of the workers, the peasants and the revolutionary intellectuals. Under the rule of the Khrushchov clique, there is no democracy for the Soviet working people, there is democracy only for the handful of people belonging to the revisionist Khrushchov clique, for the privileged stratum and for the bourgeois elements, old and new. Khrushchov's "democracy for the whole people" is nothing but out-and-out bourgeois democracy, *i.e.*, a despotic dictatorship of the Khrushchov clique over the Soviet people.

In the Soviet Union today, anyone who persists in the proletarian stand, upholds Marxism-Leninism and has the courage to speak out, to resist or to fight is watched, followed, summoned, and even arrested, imprisoned or diagnosed as "mentally ill" and sent to "mental hospitals." Recently the Soviet press has declared that it is necessary to "fight" against those who show even the slightest dissatisfaction, and called for "relentless battle" against the "rotten jokers"[45] who are so bold as to make sarcastic remarks about Khrushchov's agricultural policy. It is par-

[45] *Izvestia,* March 10, 1964.

ticularly astonishing that the revisionist Khrushchov clique should have on more than one occasion bloodily suppressed striking workers and the masses who put up resistance.

The formula of abolishing the dictatorship of the proletariat while keeping a state of the whole people reveals the secret of the revisionist Khrushchov clique; that is, they are firmly opposed to the dictatorship of the proletariat but will not give up state power till their doom. The revisionist Khrushchov clique know the paramount importance of controlling state power. They need the state machinery for repressing the Soviet working people and the Marxist-Leninists. They need it for clearing the way for the restoration of capitalism in the Soviet Union. These are Khrushchov's real aims in raising the banners of the "state of the whole people" and "democracy for the whole people."

REFUTATION OF THE SO-CALLED PARTY
OF THE ENTIRE PEOPLE

At the 22nd Congress of the CPSU Khrushchov openly raised another banner, the alteration of the proletarian character of the Communist Party of the Soviet Union. He announced the replacement of the party of the proletariat by a "party of the entire people." The programme of the CPSU states, "As a result of the victory of socialism in the U.S.S.R. and the consolidation of the unity of Soviet society, the Communist Party of the working class has become the vanguard of the Soviet people, a party of the entire people." The Open Letter of the Central Committee of the CPSU says that the CPSU "has become a political organization of the entire people."

How absurd!

1. On Khrushchov's Phoney Communism

Elementary knowledge of Marxism-Leninism tells us that, like the state, a political party is an instrument of class struggle. Every political party has a class character. Party spirit is the concentrated expression of class character. There is no such thing as a non-class or supra-class political party and there never has been, nor is there such a thing as a "party of the entire people" that does not represent the interests of a particular class.

The party of the proletariat is built in accordance with the revolutionary theory and revolutionary style of Marxism-Leninism; it is the party formed by the advanced elements who are boundlessly faithful to the historical mission of the proletariat, it is the organized vanguard of the proletariat and the highest form of its organization. The party of the proletariat represents the interests of the proletariat and the concentration of its will.

Moreover, the party of the proletariat is the only party able to represent the interests of the people, who constitute over ninety per cent of the total population. The reason is that the interests of the proletariat are identical with those of the working masses, that the proletarian party can approach problems in the light of the historical role as the proletariat and in terms of the present and future interests of the proletariat and the working masses and of the best interests of the overwhelming majority of the people, and that it can give correct leadership in accordance with Marxism-Leninism.

In addition to its members of working-class origin, the party of the proletariat has members of other class origins. But the latter do not join the Party as representatives of other classes. From the very day they join the Party they must abandon their former class stand and take the stand of the proletariat. Marx and Engels said:

1. On Khrushchov's Phoney Communism

If people of this kind from other classes join the proletarian movement, the first condition must be that they should not bring any remnants of bourgeois, petty-bourgeois, etc., prejudices with them but should wholeheartedly adopt the proletarian outlook.[46]

The basic principles concerning the character of the proletarian party were long ago elucidated by Marxism-Leninism. But in the opinion of the revisionist Khrushchov clique these principles are "stereotyped formulas," while their "party of the entire people" conforms to the "actual dialectics of the development of the Communist Party."[47]

The revisionist Khrushchov clique have cudgelled their brains to think up arguments justifying their "party of the entire people." They have argued during the talks between the Chinese and Soviet Parties in July 1963 and in the Soviet press that they have changed the Communist Party of the Soviet Union into a "party of the entire people" because:

1. The CPSU expresses the interests of the whole people.

2. The entire people have accepted the Marxist-Leninist world outlook of the working class, and the aim of the working class—the building of communism—has become the aim of the entire people.

3. The ranks of the CPSU consist of the best representatives of the workers, collective farmers and intel-

---

[46] "Marx and Engels to A. Bebel, W. Liebknecht, W. Bracke and Others ("Circular Letter"), Sept. 17-18, 1879," *Selected Works of Marx and Engels*, FLPH, Moscow, Vol. 2, pp. 484-85.

[47] "From the Party of the Working Class to the Party of the Whole Soviet People," editorial board's article of *Partyinaya Zhizn*, Moscow, No. 8, 1964.

lectuals. The CPSU unites in its own ranks representatives of over a hundred nationalities and peoples.

4. The democratic method used in the Party's activities is also in accord with its character as the Party of the entire people.

It is obvious even at a glance that none of these arguments adduced by the revisionist Khrushchov clique shows a serious approach to a serious problem.

When Lenin was fighting the opportunist muddleheads, he remarked:

> Can people obviously incapable of taking serious problems seriously, themselves be taken seriously? It is difficult to do so, comrades, very difficult! But the question which certain people cannot treat seriously is in itself so serious that it will do no harm to examine even patently frivolous replies to it.[48]

Today, too, it will do no harm to examine the patently frivolous replies given by the revisionist Khrushchov clique to so serious a question as that of the party of the proletariat.

According to the revisionist Khrushchov clique, the Communist Party should become a "party of the entire people" because it expresses the interests of the entire people. Does it not then follow that from the very beginning it should have been a "party of the entire people" instead of a party of the proletariat?

According to the revisionist Khrushchov clique, the Communist Party should become a "party of the entire people" because "the entire people have accepted the Marxist-Leninist world outlook of the working class." But

[48] Lenin, "Clarity First and Foremost," *Collected Works*, FLPH, Moscow, 1964, Vol. 20, p. 544.

how can it be said that everyone has accepted the Marxist-Leninist world outlook in Soviet society where sharp class polarization and class struggle are taking place? Can it be said that the tens of thousands of old and new bourgeois elements in your country are all Marxist-Leninists? If Marxism-Leninism has really become the world outlook of the entire people, as you allege, does it not then follow that there is no difference in your society between Party and non-Party and no need whatsoever for the Party to exist? What difference does it make if there is a "party of the entire people" or not?

According to the revisionist Khrushchov clique, the Communist Party should become a "party of the entire people" because its membership consists of workers, peasants and intellectuals and all nationalities and peoples. Does this mean then that before the idea of the "party of the entire people" was put forward at its 22nd Congress none of the members of the CPSU came from classes other than the working class? Does it mean that formerly the members of the Party all came from just one nationality, to the exclusion of other nationalities and peoples? If the character of a party is determined by the social background of its membership, does it not then follow that the numerous political parties in the world whose members also come from various classes, nationalities and peoples are all "parties of the entire people"?

According to the revisionist Khrushchov clique, the Party should be a "party of the entire people" because the methods it uses in its activities are democratic. But from its outset, a Communist Party is built on the basis of the principle of democratic centralism and should always adopt the mass line and the democratic method of persuasion and education in working among the people. Does it not then follow that a Communist Party is a "party of the entire people" from the first day of its founding?

Briefly, none of the arguments listed by the revisionist Khrushchov clique holds water.

Besides making a great fuss about a "party of the entire people," Khrushchov has also divided the Party into an "industrial Party" and an "agricultural Party" on the pretext of "building the Party organs on the production principle."[49]

The revisionist Khrushchov clique say that they have done so because of "the primacy of economics over politics under socialism"[50] and because they want to place "the economic and production problems, which have been pushed to the forefront by the entire course of the communist construction, at the centre of the activities of the Party organizations" and make them "the cornerstone of all their work."[51] Khrushchov said, "We say bluntly that the main thing in the work of the Party organs is production."[52] And what is more, they have foisted these views on Lenin, claiming that they are acting in accordance with his principles.

However, anyone at all acquainted with the history of the CPSU knows that, far from being Lenin's views, they are anti-Leninist views and that they were views held by Trotsky. On this question, too, Khrushchov is a worthy disciple of Trotsky.

[49] N. S. Khrushchov, Report at the Plenary Meeting of the Central Committee of the CPSU, Nov. 1962.

[50] "Study, Know, Act," editorial of *Economicheskaya Gazeta*, No. 50, 1962.

[51] "The Communist and Production," editorial of *Kommunist*. No. 2, 1963.

[52] N. S. Khrushchov, Speech at the Election Meeting of the Kalinin Constituency of Moscow, Feb. 27, 1963.

1. On Khrushchov's Phoney Communism

In criticizing Trotsky and Bukharin, Lenin said:

> Politics are the concentrated expression of economics.
> . . . Politics cannot but have precedence over economics.
> To argue differently means forgetting the A B C of
> Marxism.

He continued:

> . . . without a proper political approach to the subject
> the given class cannot maintain its rule, and *conse-*
> *quently* cannot solve *its own production problems*.[53]

The facts are crystal clear: the real purpose of the revisionist Khrushchov clique in proposing a "party of the
entire people" was completely to alter the proletarian
character of the CPSU and transform the Marxist-Leninist Party into a revisionist party.

The great Communist Party of the Soviet Union is confronted with the grave danger of degenerating from a
party of the proletariat into a party of the bourgeoisie and
from a Marxist-Leninist into a revisionist party.

Lenin said:

> A party that wants to exist cannot allow the slightest
> wavering on the question of its existence or any agree-
> ment with those who may bury it.[54]

At present, the revisionist Khrushchov clique is again
confronting the broad membership of the great Communist Party of the Soviet Union with precisely this serious
question.

[53] Lenin, "Once Again on the Trade Unions, the Present Situation and the Mistakes of Trotsky and Bukharin," *Selected Works*,
International Publishers, New York, 1943, Vol. 9, pp. 54 and 55.

[54] Lenin, "How Vera Zasulich Demolishes Liquidationism," *Collected Works*, FLPH, Moscow, 1963, Vol. 19, p. 414.

1. On Khrushchov's Phoney Communism

At the 22nd Congress of the CPSU, Khrushchov announced that the Soviet Union had already entered the period of the extensive building of communist society. He also declared that "we shall, in the main, have built a communist society within twenty years."[55] This is pure fraud.

How can there be talk of building communism when the revisionist Khrushchov clique are leading the Soviet Union onto the path of the restoration of capitalism and when the Soviet people are in grave danger of losing the fruits of socialism?

In putting up the signboard of "building communism" Khrushchov's real aim is to conceal the true face of his revisionism. But it is not hard to expose this trick. Just as the eyeball of a fish cannot be allowed to pass as a pearl, so revisionism cannot be allowed to pass itself off as communism.

Scientific communism has a precise and definite meaning. According to Marxism-Leninism, communist society is a society in which classes and class differences are completely eliminated, the entire people have a high level of communist consciousness and morality as well as boundless enthusiasm for and initiative in labor, there is a great abundance of social products and the principle of "from each according to his ability, to each according to his needs" is applied, and in which the state has withered away.

Marx declared:

In the higher phase of communist society, after the

[55] N. S. Khrushchov, "On the Programme of the Communist Party of the Soviet Union," at the 22nd Congress of the CPSU in Oct. 1961.

enslaving subordination of the individual to the division of labor, and therewith also the antithesis between mental and physical labor, has vanished; after labor has become not only a means of life but life's prime want; after the productive forces have also increased with the all-round development of the individual, and all the springs of co-operative wealth flow more abundantly—only then can the narrow horizon of bourgeois right be crossed in its entirety and society inscribe on its banners: From each according to his ability, to each according to his needs![56]

According to Marxist-Leninist theory, the purpose of upholding the dictatorship of the proletariat in the period of socialism is precisely to ensure that society develops in the direction of communism. Lenin said that "forward development, i.e., towards Communism, proceeds through the dictatorship of the proletariat, and cannot do otherwise."[57] Since the revisionist Khrushchov clique have abandoned the dictatorship of the proletariat in the Soviet Union, it is going backward and not forward, going backward to capitalism and not forward to communism.

Going forward to communism means moving towards the abolition of all classes and class differences. A communist society which preserves any classes at all, let alone exploiting classes, is inconceivable. Yet Khrushchov is fostering a new bourgeoisie, restoring and extending the system of exploitation and accelerating class polarization in the Soviet Union. A privileged bourgeois stratum opposed to the Soviet people now occupies the ruling posi-

[56] Marx, "Critique of the Gotha Programme," *Selected Works of Marx and Engels*, FLPH, Moscow, Vol. 2, p. 24.

[57] Lenin, "The State and Revolution," *Selected Works*, FLPH, Moscow, Vol. 2, Part 1, p. 291.

tion in the Party and government and in the economic, cultural and other departments. Can one find an iota of communism in all this?

Going forward to communism means moving towards a unitary system of the ownership of the means of production by the whole people. A communist society in which several kinds of ownership of the means of production co-exist is inconceivable. Yet Khrushchov is creating a situation in which enterprises owned by the whole people are gradually degenerating into capitalist enterprises and farms under the system of collective ownership are gradually degenerating into units of a kulak economy. Again, can one find an iota of communism in all this?

Going forward to communism means moving towards a great abundance of social products and the realization of the principle of "from each according to his ability, to each according to his needs." A communist society built on the enrichment of a handful of persons and the impoverishment of the masses is inconceivable. Under the socialist system the great Soviet people developed the social productive forces at unprecedented speed. But the evils of Khrushchov's revisionism are creating havoc in the Soviet socialist economy. Constantly beset with innumerable contradictions, Khrushchov makes frequent changes in his economic policies and often goes back on his own words, thus throwing the Soviet national economy into a state of chaos. Khrushchov is truly an incorrigible wastrel. He has squandered the grain reserves built up under Stalin and brought great difficulties into the lives of the Soviet people. He has distorted and violated the socialist principle of distribution of "from each according to his ability, to each according to his work," and enabled a handful of persons to appropriate the fruits of the labor of the broad masses of the Soviet people. These points alone are sufficient to prove that the road taken by Khrushchov leads away from communism.

Going forward to communism means moving towards enhancing the communist consciousness of the masses. A communist society with bourgeois ideas running rampant is inconceivable. Yet Khrushchov is zealously reviving bourgeois ideology in the Soviet Union and serving as a missionary for the decadent American culture. By propagating material incentive, he is turning all human relations into money relations and encouraging individualism and selfishness. Because of him, manual labor is again considered sordid and love of pleasure at the expense of other people's labor is again considered honorable. Certainly, the social ethics and atmosphere promoted by Khrushchov are far removed from communism, as far as far can be.

Going forward to communism means moving towards the withering away of the state. A communist society with a state apparatus for oppressing the people is inconceivable. The state of the dictatorship of the proletariat is actually no longer a state in its original sense, because it is no longer a machine used by the exploiting few to oppress the overwhelming majority of the people but a machine for exercising dictatorship over a very small number of exploiters, while democracy is practised among the overwhelming majority of the people. Khrushchov is altering the character of Soviet state power and changing the dictatorship of the proletariat back into an instrument whereby a handful of privileged bourgeois elements exercise dictatorship over the mass of the Soviet workers, peasants and intellectuals. He is continuously strengthening his dictatorial state apparatus and intensifying his repression of the Soviet people. It is indeed a great mockery to talk about communism in these circumstances.

A comparison of all this with the principles of scientific communism readily reveals that in every respect the revisionist Khrushchov clique are leading the Soviet Union away from the path of socialism and onto the path of capitalism and, as a consequence, further and further away from, instead of closer to, the communist goal of "from each according to his ability, to each according to his needs."

Khrushchov has ulterior motives when he puts up the signboard of communism. He is using it to fool the Soviet people and cover up his effort to restore capitalism. He is using it to deceive the international proletariat and the revolutionary people the world over and betray proletarian internationalism. Under this signboard, the Khrushchov clique has itself abandoned proletarian internationalism and is seeking a partnership with U.S. imperialism for the partition of the world; moreover, it wants the fraternal socialist countries to serve its own private interests and not to oppose imperialism or to support the revolutions of the oppressed peoples and nations, and it wants them to accept its political, economic and military control and be its virtual dependencies and colonies. Furthermore, the Khrushchov clique wants all the oppressed peoples and nations to serve its private interests and abandon their revolutionary struggles, so as not to disturb its sweet dream of partnership with imperialism for the division of the world, and instead submit to enslavement and oppression by imperialism and its lackeys.

In short, Khrushchov's slogan of basically "building a communist society within twenty years" in the Soviet Union is not only false but also reactionary.

1. On Khrushchov's Phoney Communism

The revisionist Khrushchov clique say that the Chinese "go to the length of questioning the very right of our Party and people to build communism."[58] This is a despicable attempt to fool the Soviet people and poison the friendship of the Chinese and Soviet people. We have never had any doubt that the great Soviet people will eventually enter into communist society. But right now the revisionist Khrushchov clique are damaging the socialist fruits of the Soviet people and taking away their right to go forward to communism. In the circumstances, the issue confronting the Soviet people is not how to build communism but rather how to resist and oppose Khrushchov's effort to restore capitalism.

The revisionist Khrushchov clique also say that "the CPC leaders hint that, since our Party has made its aim a better life for the people, Soviet society is being bourgeoisified," is 'degenerating.' "[59] This trick of deflecting the Soviet people's dissatisfaction with the Khrushchov clique is deplorable as well as stupid. We sincerely wish the Soviet people an increasingly better life. But Khrushchov's boasts of "concern for the well-being of the people" and of "a better life for every man" are utterly false and demagogic. For the masses of the Soviet people life is already bad enough at Khrushchov's hands. The Khrushchov clique seek a "better life" only for the members of the privileged stratum and the bourgeois elements, old and new, in the Soviet Union. These people are appropriating the fruits of the Soviet people's labor and living the life of

[58] M. A. Suslov, Report at the Plenary Meeting of the Central Committee of the CPSU, Feb. 1964.

[59] "Open Letter of the Central Committee of the Communist Party of the Soviet Union to Party Organizations and All Communists in the Soviet Union," July 14, 1963.

1. On Khrushchov's Phoney Communism

bourgeois lords. They have indeed become thoroughly bourgeoisified.

Khrushchov's "communism" is in essence a variant of bourgeois socialism. He does not regard communism as completely abolishing classes and class differences but describes it as "a bowl accessible to all and brimming with the products of physical and mental labor."[60] He does not regard the struggle of the working class for communism as a struggle for the thorough emancipation of all mankind as well as itself but describes it as a struggle for "a good dish of goulash." There is not an iota of scientific communism in his head but only the image of a society of bourgeois philistines.

Khrushchov's "communism" takes the United States for its model. Imitation of the methods of management of U. S. capitalism and the bourgeois way of life has been raised by Khrushchov to the level of state policy. He says that he "always thinks highly" of the achievements of the United States. He "rejoices in these achievements, is a little envious at times."[61] He extols to the sky a letter by Roswell Garst, a big U. S. farmer, which propagates the capitalist system;[62] actually he has taken it as his agricultural programme. He wants to copy the United States in the sphere of industry as well as that of agriculture and, in particular, to imitate the profit motive of U. S. capitalist enterprises. He shows great admiration for the American way of life, asserting that the American people "do not

[60] N. S. Khrushchov, Speech for the Austrian Radio and Television, July 7, 1960.

[61] N. S. Khrushchov, Interview with Leaders of U.S. Congress and Members of the Senate Foreign Relations Committee, Sept. 16, 1959.

[62] N. S. Khrushchov, Speech at the Plenary Meeting of the Central Committee of the CPSU, Feb. 1964.

live badly"[63] under the rule and enslavement of monopoly capital. Going further, Khrushchov is hopeful of building communism with loans from U.S. imperialism. During his visits to the United States and Hungary, he expressed on more than one occasion his readiness "to take credits from the devil himself."

Thus it can be seen that Khrushchov's "communism" is indeed "goulash communism," the "communism of the American way of life" and "communism seeking credits from the devil." No wonder he often tells representatives of Western monopoly capital that once such "communism" is realized in the Soviet Union, "you will go forward to communism without any call from me."[64]

There is nothing new about such "communism." It is simply another name for capitalism. It is only a bourgeois label, sign or advertisement. In ridiculing the old-line revisionist parties which set up the signboard of Marxism, Lenin said:

> Wherever Marxism is popular among the workers, this political tendency, this "bourgeois labor party," will swear by the name of Marx. It cannot be prohibited from doing this, just as a trading firm cannot be prohibited from using any particular label, sign, or advertisement.[65]

It is thus easily understandable why Khrushchov's "communism" is appreciated by imperialism and monopoly capital. The U.S. Secretary of State Dean Rusk has said:

[63] N. S. Khrushchov, Talk at a Meeting with Businessman and Public Leaders in Pittsburgh, U.S.A., Sept. 24, 1959.

[64] N. S. Khrushchov, Talk at a Meeting with French Parliamentarians, March 25, 1960.

[65] Lenin, "Imperialism and the Split in Socialism," *Selected Works*, International Publishers, New York, Vol. 11, p. 761.

1. On Khrushchov's Phoney Communism

. . . to the extent that goulash and the second pair of trousers and questions of that sort become more important in the Soviet Union, I think to that extent a moderating influence has come into the present scene.[66]

And the British Prime Minister Douglas-Home has said:

Mr. Khrushchov said that the Russian brand of communism puts education and goulash first. That is good; goulash-communism is better than war-communism, and I am glad to have this confirmation of our view that fat and comfortable Communists are better than lean and hungry Communists.[67]

Khrushchov's revisionism entirely caters to the policy of "peaceful evolution" which U.S. imperialism is pursuing with regard to the Soviet Union and other socialist countries. John Foster Dulles said:

. . . there was evidence within the Soviet Union of forces toward greater liberalism which, if they persisted, could bring about a basic change within the Soviet Union.[68]

The liberal forces Dulles talked about are capitalist forces. The basic change Dulles hoped for is the degeneration of socialism into capitalism. Khrushchov is effecting exactly the "basic change" Dulles dreamed of.

How the imperialists are hoping for the restoration of capitalism in the Soviet Union! How they are rejoicing!

We would advise the imperialist lords not to be happy too soon. Notwithstanding all the services of the revi-

[66] Dean Rusk, Interview on British Broadcasting Corporation Television, May 10, 1964.
[67] A. Douglas-Home, Speech at Norwich, England, April 6, 1964.
[68] J. F. Dulles, press conference, May 15, 1956.

sionist Khrushchov clique, nothing can save imperialism from its doom. The revisionist ruling clique suffer from the same kind of disease as the imperialist ruling clique; they are extremely antagonistic to the masses of the people who comprise over ninety per cent of the world's population, and therefore they, too, are weak and powerless and are paper tigers. Like the clay Buddha that tried to wade across the river, the revisionist Khrushchov clique cannot even save themselves, so how can they endow imperialism with long life?

HISTORICAL LESSONS OF THE DICTATORSHIP OF THE PROLETARIAT

Khrushchov's revisionism has inflicted heavy damage on the international communist movement, but at the same time it has educated the Marxist-Leninists and revolutionary people throughout the world by negative example.

If it may be said that the Great October Revolution provided Marxist-Leninists in all countries with the most important positive experience and opened up the road for the proletarian seizure of political power, then on its part Khrushchov's revisionism may be said to have provided them with the most important negative experience, enabling Marxist-Leninists in all countries to draw the appropriate lessons for preventing the degeneration of the proletarian party and the socialist state.

Historically all revolutions have had their reverses and their twists and turns. Lenin once asked:

> . . . if we take the matter in its essence, has it ever happened in history that a new mode of production

took root immediately, without a long succession of setbacks, blunders and relapses?[69]

The international proletarian revolution has a history of less than a century counting from 1871 when the proletariat of the Paris Commune made the first heroic attempt at the seizure of political power, or barely half a century counting from the October Revolution. The proletarian revolution, the greatest revolution in human history, replaces capitalism by socialism and private ownership by public ownership and uproots all the systems of exploitation and all the exploiting classes. It is all the more natural that so earth-shaking a revolution should have to go through serious and fierce class struggles, inevitably traverse a long and tortuous course beset with reverses.

History furnishes a number of examples in which proletarian rule suffered defeat as a result of armed suppression by the bourgeoisie, for instance, the Paris Commune and the Hungarian Soviet Republic of 1919. In contemporary times, too, there was the counter-revolutionary rebellion in Hungary in 1956, when the rule of the proletariat was almost overthrown. People can easily perceive this form of capitalist restoration and are more alert and watchful against it.

However, they cannot easily perceive and are often off their guard or not vigilant against another form of capitalist restoration, which therefore presents a greater danger. The state of the dictatorship of the proletariat takes the road of revisionism or the road of "peaceful evolution" as a result of the degeneration of the leadership of the Party and the state. A lesson of this kind was provided some years ago by the revisionist Tito clique who brought

[69] Lenin, "A Great Beginning," *Selected Works*, FLPH, Moscow, Vol. 2, Part 2, p. 229.

about the degeneration of socialist Yugoslavia into a capitalist country. But the Yugoslav lesson alone has not sufficed to arouse people's attention fully. Some may say that perhaps it was an accident.

But now the revisionist Khrushchov clique have usurped the leadership of the Party and the state, and there is grave danger of a restoration of capitalism in the Soviet Union, the land of the Great October Revolution with its history of several decades in building socialism. And this sounds the alarm for all socialist countries, including China, and for all the Communist and Workers' Parties, including the Communist Party of China. Inevitably it arouses very great attention and forces Marxist-Leninists and revolutionary people the world over to ponder deeply and sharpen their vigilance.

The emergence of Khrushchov's revisionism is a bad thing, and it is also a good thing. So long as the countries where socialism has been achieved and also those that will later embark on the socialist road seriously study the lessons of the "peaceful evolution" promoted by the revisionist Khrushchov clique and take the appropriate measures, they will be able to prevent this kind of "peaceful evolution" as well as crush the enemy's armed attacks. Thus, the victory of the world proletarian revolution will be more certain.

The Communist Party of China has a history of forty-three years. During its protracted revolutionary struggle, our Party combated both Right and "Left" opportunist errors and the Marxist-Leninist leadership of the Central Committee headed by Comrade Mao Tse-tung was established. Closely integrating the universal truth of Marxism-Leninism with the concrete practice of revolution and construction in China, Comrade Mao Tse-tung has led the

Chinese people from victory to victory. The Central Committee of the Chinese Communist Party and Comrade Mao Tse-tung have taught us to wage unremitting struggle in the theoretical, political and organizational fields, as well as in practical work, so as to combat revisionism and prevent a restoration of capitalism. The Chinese people have gone through protracted revolutionary armed struggles and possess a glorious revolutionary tradition. The Chinese People's Liberation Army is armed with Mao Tse-tung's thinking and inseparably linked to the masses. The numerous cadres of the Chinese Communist Party have been educated and tempered in rectification movements and sharp class struggles. All these factors make it very difficult to restore capitalism in our country.

But let us look at the facts. Is our society today thoroughly clean? No, it is not. Classes and class struggle still remain, the activities of the overthrown reactionary classes plotting a comeback still continue, and we still have speculative activities by old and new bourgeois elements and desperate forays by embezzlers, grafters and degenerates. There are also cases of degeneration in a few primary organizations; what is more, these degenerates do their utmost to find protectors and agents in the higher leading bodies. We should not in the least slacken our vigilance against such phenomena but must keep fully alert.

The struggle in the socialist countries between the road of socialism and the road of capitalism—between the forces of capitalism attempting a comeback and the forces opposing it—is unavoidable. But the restoration of capitalism in the socialist countries and their degeneration into capitalist countries are certainly not unavoidable. We can prevent the restoration of capitalism so long as there is a correct leadership and a correct understanding of the problem, so long as we adhere to the revolutionary Marxist-Leninist line, take the appropriate measures and wage a prolonged, unremitting struggle. The struggle between the socialist and capitalist roads can become a driving force for social advance.

How can the restoration of capitalism be prevented? On this question Comrade Mao Tse-tung has formulated a set of theories and policies, after summing up the practical experience of the dictatorship of the proletariat in China and studying the positive and negative experience of other countries, mainly of the Soviet Union, in accordance with the basic principles of Marxism-Leninism, and has thus enriched and developed the Marxist-Leninist theory of the dictatorship of the proletariat.

The main contents of the theories and policies advanced by Comrade Mao Tse-tung in this connection are as follows:

FIRST, it is necessary to apply the Marxist-Leninist law of the unity of opposites to the study of socialist society. The law of contradiction in all things, *i.e.*, the law of the unity of opposites, is the fundamental law of materialist dialectics. It operates everywhere, whether in the natural world, in human society, or in human thought. The opposites in a contradiction both unite and struggle with each other, and it is this that forces things to move and change. Socialist society is no exception. In socialist society there are two kinds of social contradictions, namely, the contradictions among the people and those between ourselves and the enemy. These two kinds of social contradictions are entirely different in their essence, and the methods for handling them should be different, too. Their correct handling will result in the increasing consolidation of the dictatorship of the proletariat and the further strengthening and development of socialist society. Many people acknowledge the law of the unity of opposites but are unable to apply it in studying and handling questions in socialist society. They refuse to admit that there are contradictions in socialist society—that there are not only contradictions between ourselves and the enemy but also contradictions among the people—and they do not know how to distinguish between these two kinds of social contradictions and how to handle them correctly, and are therefore unable to deal correctly with the question of the dictatorship of the proletariat.

SECOND, socialist society covers a very long historical period. Classes and class struggle continue to exist in this society, and the struggle still goes on between the road of socialism and the road of capitalism. The socialist revolution on the economic front (in the ownership of the means of production) is insufficient by itself and cannot be consolidated. There must also be a thorough socialist revolution on the political and ideological fronts. Here a very long period of time is needed to decide "who will win" in the struggle between socialism and capitalism. Several decades won't do it; success requires anywhere from one to several centuries. On the question of duration, it is better to prepare for a longer rather than a shorter period of time. On the question of effort, it is better to regard the task as difficult rather than easy. It will be more advantageous and less harmful to think and act in this way. Anyone who fails to see this or to appreciate it fully will make tremendous mistakes. During the historical period of socialism it is necessary to maintain the dictatorship of the proletariat and carry the socialist revolution through to the end if the restoration of capitalism is to be prevented, socialist construction carried forward and the conditions created for the transition to communism.

THIRD, the dictatorship of the proletariat is led by the working class, with the worker-peasant alliance as its basis. This means the exercise of dictatorship by the working class and by the people under its leadership over the reactionary classes and individuals and those elements who oppose socialist transformation and socialist construction. Within the ranks of the people democratic centralism is practised. Ours is the broadest democracy beyond the bounds of possibility for any bourgeois state.

FOURTH, in both socialist revolution and socialist construction it is necessary to adhere to the mass line, boldly to arouse the masses and to unfold mass movements on a large scale. The mass line of "from the masses, to the masses" is the basic line in all the work of our Party. It is necessary to have firm confidence in the majority of the people and, above all, in the majority of the worker-peasant masses. We must be good at consulting the masses in our work and under no circumstances alienate ourselves from them. Both commandism and the attitude of one dispensing favors have to be fought. The full and frank expression of views and great debates are important forms of revolutionary struggle which have been created by the people of our country in the course of their long revolutionary fight, forms of struggle which rely on the masses for resolving contradictions among the people and contradictions between ourselves and the enemy.

FIFTH, whether in socialist revolution or in socialist construction, it is necessary to solve the question of whom to rely on, whom to win over and whom to oppose. The proletariat and its vanguard must make a class analysis of socialist society, rely on the truly dependable forces that firmly take the socialist road, win over all allies that can be won over, and unite with the masses of the people, who constitute more than ninety-five per cent of the population, in a common struggle against the enemies of socialism. In the rural areas, after the collectivization of agriculture it is necessary to rely on the poor and lower middle peasants in order to consolidate the dictatorship of the proletariat and the worker-peasant alliance, defeat the spontaneous capitalist tendencies and constantly strengthen and extend the positions of socialism.

SIXTH, it is necessary to conduct extensive socialist education movements repeatedly in the cities and the countryside. In these continuous movements for educating the people we must be good at organizing the revolutionary class forces, enhancing their class consciousness, correctly handling contradictions among the people and uniting all those who can be united. In these movements it is necessary to wage a sharp, tit-for-tat struggle against the anti-socialist, capitalist and feudal forces—the landlords, rich peasants, counter-revolutionaries and bourgeois rightists, and the embezzlers, grafters and degenerates—in order to smash the attacks they unleash against socialism and to remould the majority of them into new men.

SEVENTH, one of the basic tasks of the dictatorship of the proletariat is actively to expand the socialist economy. It is necessary to achieve the modernization of industry, agriculture, science and technology, and national defence step by step under the guidance of the general policy of developing the national economy with agriculture as the foundation and industry as the leading factor. On the basis of the growth of production, it is necessary to raise the living standards of the people gradually and on a broad scale.

1. On Khrushchov's Phoney Communism

EIGHTH, ownership by the whole people and collective ownership are the two forms of socialist economy. The transition from collective ownership to ownership by the whole people, from two kinds of ownership to a unitary ownership by the whole people, is a rather long process. Collective ownership itself develops from lower to higher levels and from smaller to larger scale. The people's commune which the Chinese people have created is a suitable form of organization for the solution of the question of this transition.

NINTH, "Let a hundred flowers blossom and a hundred schools of thought contend" is a policy for stimulating the growth of the arts and the progress of science and for promoting a flourishing socialist culture. Education must serve proletarian politics and must be combined with productive labor. The working people should master knowledge and the intellectuals should become habituated to manual labor. Among those engaged in science, culture, the arts and education, the struggle to promote proletarian ideology and destroy bourgeois ideology is a protracted and fierce class struggle. It is necessary to build up a large detachment of working-class intellectuals who serve socialism and who are both "red and expert," *i.e.*, who are both politically conscious and professionally competent, by means of the cultural revolution, and revolutionary practice in class struggle, the struggle for production and scientific experiment.

TENTH, it is necessary to maintain the system of cadre participation in collective productive labor. The cadres of our Party and state are ordinary workers and not overlords sitting on the backs of the people. By taking part in collective productive labor, the cadres maintain extensive, constant and close ties with the working people. This is a major measure of fundamental importance for a socialist system; it helps to overcome bureaucracy and to prevent revisionism and dogmatism.

ELEVENTH, the system of high salaries for a small number of people should never be applied. The gap between the incomes of the working personnel of the Party, the government, the enterprises and the people's communes, on the one hand, and the incomes of the mass of the people, on the other, should be rationally and gradually narrowed and not widened. All working personnel must be prevented from abusing their power and enjoying special privileges.

TWELFTH, it is always necessary for the people's armed forces of a socialist country to be under the leadership of the Party of the proletariat and under the supervision of the masses, and they must always maintain the glorious tradition of a people's army, with unity between the army and the people and between officers and men. It is necessary to keep the system under which officers serve as common soldiers at regular intervals. It is necessary to practise military democracy, political democracy and economic democracy. Moreover, militia units should be organized and trained all over the country, so as to make everybody a soldier. The guns must forever be in the hands of the Party and the people and must never be allowed to become the instruments of careerists.

THIRTEENTH, the people's public security organs must always be under the leadership of the Party of the proletariat and under the supervision of the mass of the people. In the struggle to defend the fruits of socialism and the people's interests, the policy must be applied of relying on the combined efforts of the broad masses and the security organs, so that not a single bad person escapes

or a single good person is wronged. Counter-revolutionaries must be suppressed whenever found, and mistakes
must be corrected whenever discovered.

FOURTEENTH, in foreign policy, it is necessary to
uphold proletarian internationalism and oppose great-
power chauvinism and national egoism. The socialist
camp is the product of the struggle of the international
proletariat and working people. It belongs to the proletariat and working people of the whole world as well as
to the people of the socialist countries. We must truly put
into effect the fighting slogans, "Workers of all countries,
unite!" and "Workers and oppressed nations of the world,
unite!," resolutely combat the anti-Communist, anti-
popular and counter-revolutionary policies of imperialism
and reaction and support the revolutionary struggles of all
the oppressed classes and oppressed nations. Relations
among socialist countries should be based on the principles
of independence, complete equality and the proletarian internationalist principle of mutual support and mutual assistance. Every socialist country should rely mainly on
itself for its construction. If any socialist country practises
national egoism in its foreign policy, or, worse yet, eagerly
works in partnership with imperialism for the partition of
the world, such conduct is degenerate and a betrayal of
proletarian internationalism.

FIFTEENTH, as the vanguard of the proletariat, the
Communist Party must exist as long as the dictatorship
of the proletariat exists. The Communist Party is the
highest form of organization of the proletariat. The leading role of the proletariat is realized through the leadership of the Communist Party. The system of Party committees exercising leadership must be put into effect in all
departments. During the period of the dictatorship of the

proletariat, the proletarian party must maintain and strengthen its close ties with the proletariat and the broad masses of the working people, maintain and develop its vigorous revolutionary style, uphold the principle of integrating the universal truth of Marxism-Leninism with the concrete practice of its own country, and persist in the struggle against revisionism, dogmatism and opportunism of every kind.

In the light of the historical lessons of the dictatorship of the proletariat Comrade Mao Tse-tung has stated:

Class struggle, the struggle for production and scientific experiment are the three great revolutionary movements for building a mighty socialist country. These movements are a sure guarantee that Communists will be free from bureaucracy and immune against revisionism and dogmatism, and will forever remain invincible. They are a reliable guarantee that the proletariat will be able to unite with the broad working masses and realize a democratic dictatorship. If, in the absence of these movements, the landlords, rich peasants, counter-revolutionaries, bad elements and ogres of all kinds were allowed to crawl out, while our cadres were to shut their eyes to all this and in many cases fail even to differentiate between the enemy and ourselves but were to collaborate with the enemy and become corrupted and demoralized, if our cadres were thus dragged into the enemy camp or the enemy were able to sneak into our ranks, and if many of our workers, peasants, and intellectuals were left defenceless against both the soft and the hard tactics of the enemy, then it would not take long, perhaps only several years or a decade, or several decades at most, before a counter-revolutionary restoration on a national scale inevitably occurred, the Marx-

ist-Leninist party would undoubtedly become a revisionist party or a fascist party, and the whole of China
would change its color.[70]

Comrade Mao Tse-tung has pointed out that, in order
to guarantee that our Party and country do not change
their color, we must not only have a correct line and correct policies but must train and bring up millions of successors who will carry on the cause of proletarian
revolution.

In the final analysis, the question of training successors
for the revolutionary cause of the proletariat is one of
whether or not there will be people who can carry on the
Marxist-Leninist revolutionary cause started by the older
generation of proletarian revolutionaries, whether or not
the leadership of our Party and state will remain in the
hands of proletarian revolutionaries, whether or not our
descendants will continue to march along the correct road
laid down by Marxism-Leninism, or, in other words,
whether or not we can successfully prevent the emergence
of Khrushchovite revisionism in China, In short, it is an
extremely important question, a matter of life and death
for our Party and our country. It is a question of fundamental importance to the proletarian revolutionary cause
for a hundred, a thousand, nay ten thousand years. Basing
themselves on the changes in the Soviet Union, the imperialist prophets are pinning their hopes of "peaceful evolution" on the third or fourth generation of the Chinese
Party. We must shatter these imperialist prophecies. From
our highest organizations down to the grass-roots, we

[70] Mao Tse-tung, Note on "The Seven Well-Written Documents
of the Chekiang Province Concerning Cadres' Participation in
Physical Labor," May 9, 1963.

must everywhere give constant attention to the training and upbringing of successors to the revolutionary cause.

What are the requirements for worthy successors to the revolutionary cause of the proletariat?

They must be genuine Marxist-Leninists and not revisionists like Khrushchov wearing the cloak of Marxism-Leninism.

They must be revolutionaries who wholeheartedly serve the majority of the people of China and the whole world, and must not be like Khrushchov who serves both the interests of the handful of members of the privileged bourgeois stratum in his own country and those of foreign imperialism and reaction.

They must be proletarian statesmen capable of uniting and working together with the overwhelming majority. Not only must they unite with those who agree with them, they must also be good at uniting with those who disagree and even with those who formerly opposed them and have since been proved wrong. But they must especially watch out for careerists and conspirators like Khrushchov and prevent such bad elements from usurping the leadership of the Party and government at any level.

They must be models in applying the Party's democratic centralism, must master the method of leadership based on the principle of "from the masses, to the masses," and must cultivate a democratic style and be good at listening to the masses. They must not be despotic like Khrushchov and violate the Party's democratic centralism, make surprise attacks on comrades or act arbitrarily and dictatorially.

They must be modest and prudent and guard against arrogance and impetuosity; they must be imbued with the spirit of self-criticism and have the courage to correct mistakes and shortcomings in their work. They must not cover up their errors like Khrushchov, and claim all the credit for themselves and shift all the blame on others.

Successors to the revolutionary cause of the proletariat come forward in mass struggles and are tempered in the great storms of revolution. It is essential to test and know cadres and choose and train successors in the long course of mass struggle.

The above series of principles advanced by Comrade Mao Tse-tung are creative developments of Marxism-Leninism, to the theoretical arsenal of which they add new weapons of decisive importance for us in preventing the restoration of capitalism. So long as we follow these principles, we can consolidate the dictatorship of the proletariat, ensure that our Party and state will never change color, successfully conduct the socialist revolution and socialist construction, help all peoples' revolutionary movements for the overthrow of imperialism and its lackeys, and guarantee the future transition from socialism to communism.

* * *

Regarding the emergence of the revisionist Khrushchov clique in the Soviet Union, our attitude as Marxist-Leninists is the same as our attitude towards any "disturbance"—first, we are against it; second, we are not afraid of it.

We did not wish it and are opposed to it, but since the revisionist Khrushchov clique have already emerged, there is nothing terrifying about them, and there is no need for alarm. The earth will continue to revolve, history will continue to move forward, the people of the world will, as always, make revolutions, and the imperialists and their lackeys will inevitably meet their doom.

The historic contributions of the great Soviet people will remain forever glorious; they can never be tarnished by the revisionist Khrushchov clique's betrayal. The broad masses of the workers, peasants, revolutionary intellectuals and Communists of the Soviet Union will eventually surmount all the obstacles in their path and march towards communism.

The Soviet people, the people of all the socialist countries and the revolutionary people the world over will certainly learn lessons from the revisionist Khrushchov clique's betrayal. In the struggle against Khrushchov's revisionism, the international communist movement has grown and will continue to grow mightier than ever before.

Marxist-Leninists have always had an attitude of revolutionary optimism towards the future of the cause of the proletarian revolution. We are profoundly convinced that the brilliant light of the dictatorship of the proletariat, of socialism and of Marxism-Leninism will shine forth over the Soviet land. The proletariat is sure to win the whole world and communism is sure to achieve complete and final victory on earth.

LONG LIVE THE VICTORY OF PEOPLE'S WAR!

In Commemoration of the 20th Anniversary of Victory in the Chinese People's War of Resistance Against Japan

BY LIN PIAO

Vice-Chairman of the Central Committee of the Communist Party of China, Vice-Premier and Minister of National Defence

The Principal Contradiction in the Period of the War of Resistance Against Japan and the Line of the Communist Party of China . . . Correctly Apply the Line and Policy of the United Front . . . Rely on the Peasants and Establish Rural Base Areas . . . Build a People's Army of a New Type . . . Carry Out the Strategy and Tactics of People's War . . . Adhere to the Policy of Self-Reliance . . . The International Significance of Comrade Mao Tse-tung's Theory of People's War . . . Defeat U.S. Imperialism and Its Lackeys by People's War . . . The Khrushchov Revisionists Are Betrayers of People's War

FULL TWENTY YEARS have elapsed since our victory in the great War of Resistance Against Japan.

2. *The Victory of People's War*

After a long period of heroic struggle, the Chinese people, under the leadership of the Communist Party of China and Comrade Mao Tse-tung, won final victory two decades ago in their war against the Japanese imperialists who had attempted to subjugate China and swallow up the whole of Asia.

The Chinese people's War of Resistance was an important part of the world war against German, Japanese and Italian fascism. The Chinese people received support from the people and the anti-fascist forces all over the world. And in their turn, the Chinese people made an important contribution to victory in the Anti-Fascist War as a whole.

Of the innumerable anti-imperialist wars waged by the Chinese people in the past hundred years, the War of Resistance Against Japan was the first to end in complete victory. It occupies an extremely important place in the annals of war, in the annals of both the revolutionary wars of the Chinese people and the wars of the oppressed nations of the world against imperialist aggression.

It was a war in which a weak semi-colonial and semi-feudal country triumphed over a strong imperialist country. For a long period after the invasion of China's northeastern provinces by the Japanese imperialists, the Kuomintang followed a policy of non-resistance. In the early stage of the War of Resistance, the Japanese imperialists exploited their military superiority to drive deep into China and occupy half her territory. In the face of the massive attacks of the aggressors and the anti-Japanese upsurge of the people throughout the country, the Kuomintang was compelled to take part in the War of Resistance, but soon afterwards it adopted the policy of passive resistance to Japan and active opposition to the Communist Party. The heavy responsibility of combating Japanese

2. The Victory of People's War

imperialism thus fell on the shoulders of the Eighth Route Army, the New Fourth Army and the people of the Liberated Areas, all led by the Communist Party. At the outbreak of the war, the Eighth Route and New Fourth Armies had only a few tens of thousands of men and suffered from extreme inferiority in both arms and equipment, and for a long time they were under the crossfire of the Japanese imperialists on the one hand and the Kuomintang troops on the other. But they grew stronger and stronger in the course of the war and became the main force in defeating Japanese imperialism.

How was it possible for a weak country finally to defeat a strong country? How was it possible for a seemingly weak army to become the main force in the war?

The basic reasons were that the War of Resistance Against Japan was a genuine people's war led by the Communist Party of China and Comrade Mao Tse-tung, a war in which the correct Marxist-Leninist political and military lines were put into effect, and that the Eighth Route and New Fourth Armies were genuine people's armies which applied the whole range of strategy and tactics of people's war as formulated by Comrade Mao Tse-tung.

Comrade Mao Tse-tung's theory of and policies for people's war have creatively enriched and developed Marxism-Leninism. The Chinese people's victory in the anti-Japanese war was a victory for people's war, for Marxism-Leninism and the thought of Mao Tse-tung.

Prior to the war against Japan, the Communist Party of China had gone through the First Revolutionary Civil War of 1924-1927 and the Second Revolutionary Civil War of 1927-1936 and summed up the experience and lessons of the successes and failures in those wars, and the leading role of Mao Tse-tung's thought had become es-

2. *The Victory of People's War*

tablished within the Party. This was the fundamental guarantee of the Party's ability to lead the Chinese people to victory in the War of Resistance.

The Chinese people's victory in the War of Resistance paved the way for their seizure of state power throughout the country. When the Kuomintang reactionaries, backed by the U.S. imperialists, launched a nation-wide civil war in 1946, the Communist Party of China and Comrade Mao Tse-tung further developed the theory of people's war, led the Chinese people in waging a people's war on a still larger scale, and in the space of a little over three years the great victory of the People's Liberation War was won, the rule of imperialism, feudalism and bureaucrat-capitalism in our country ended and the People's Republic of China founded.

The victory of the Chinese people's revolutionary war breached the imperialist front in the East, wrought a great change in the world balance of forces, and accelerated the revolutionary movement among the people of all countries. From then on, the national-liberation movement in Asia, Africa, and Latin America entered a new historical period.

Today, the U.S. imperialists are repeating on a world-wide scale the past actions of the Japanese imperialists in China and other parts of Asia. It has become an urgent necessity for the people in many countries to master and use people's war as a weapon against U.S. imperialism and its lackeys. In every conceivable way U.S. imperialism and its lackeys are trying to extinguish the revolutionary flames of people's war. The Khrushchov revisionists, fearing people's war like the plague, are heaping abuse on it. The two are colluding to prevent and sabotage people's war. In these circumstances, it is of vital practical importance to review the historical experience of the great victory of the people's war in China and to recapitulate Comrade Mao Tse-tung's theory of people's war.

THE PRINCIPAL CONTRADICTION IN THE PERIOD OF THE WAR OF RESISTANCE AGAINST JAPAN AND THE LINE OF THE COMMUNIST PARTY OF CHINA

The Communist Party of China and Comrade Mao Tse-tung were able to lead the Chinese people to victory in the War of Resistance Against Japan primarily because they formulated and applied a Marxist-Leninist line.

Basing himself on the fundamental tenets of Marxism-Leninism and applying the method of class analysis, Comrade Mao Tse-tung analyzed: first, the mutual transformation of China's principal and non-principal contradictions following the invasion of China by Japanese imperialism; second, the consequent changes in class relations within China and in international relations, and, third, the balance of forces as between China and Japan. This analysis provided the scientific basis upon which the political and military lines of the War of Resistance were formulated.

There had long been two basic contradictions in China —the contradiction between imperialism and the Chinese nation, and the contradiction between feudalism and the masses of the people. For ten years before the outbreak of the War of Resistance, the Kuomintang reactionary clique, which represented the interests of imperialism, the big landlords and the big bourgeoisie, had waged civil war against the Communist Party of China and the Communist-led Workers' and Peasants' Red Army, which represented the interests of the Chinese people. In 1931, Japanese imperialism invaded and occupied northeastern China. Subsequently, and especially after 1935, it stepped

2. The Victory of People's War

up and expanded its aggression against China, penetrating deeper and deeper into our territory. As a result of its invasion, Japanese imperialism sharpened its contradiction with the Chinese nation to an extreme degree and brought about changes in class relations within China. To end the civil war and to unite against Japanese aggression became the pressing nation-wide demand of the people. Changes of varying degrees also occurred in the political attitudes of the national bourgeoisie and the various factions within the Kuomintang. And the Sian Incident[1] of 1936 was the best case in point.

How was one to assess the changes in China's political situation, and what conclusion was to be drawn? This question had a direct bearing on the very survival of the Chinese nation.

For a period prior to the outbreak of the War of Resistance, the "Left" opportunists represented by Wang Ming within the Chinese Communist Party were blind to the important changes in China's political situation caused by Japanese aggression since 1931 and denied the sharpening of the Sino-Japanese national contradiction and the demands of various social strata for a war of resistance; instead, they stressed that all the counter-revolutionary fac-

[1] Under the influence of the Chinese Workers' and Peasants' Red Army and the people's anti-Japanese movement, the Kuomintang Northeastern Army under Chang Hsueh-liang and the Kuomintang 17th Route Army under Yang Hu-cheng agreed to the anti-Japanese national united front proposed by the Communist Party of China and demanded that Chiang Kai-shek should stop the civil war and unite with the Communist Party to resist Japan. Chiang Kai-shek refused. On December 12, 1936, Chang Hsueh-liang and Yang Hu-cheng arrested him in Sian. Proceeding from the interest of the entire nation, the Chinese Communist Party offered mediation and Chiang Kai-shek was compelled to accept the terms of unity with the Communist Party and resistance to Japan.

2. The Victory of People's War

tions and intermediate forces in China and all the imperialist countries were a monolithic bloc. They persisted in their line of "closed-doorism" and continued to advocate, "Down with the whole lot."

Comrade Mao Tse-tung resolutely fought the "Left" opportunist errors and penetratingly analyzed the new situation in the Chinese revolution.

He pointed out that the Japanese imperialist attempt to reduce China to a Japanese colony heightened the contradiction between China and Japan and made it the principal contradiction; that China's internal class contradictions—such as those between the masses of the people and feudalism, between the peasantry and the landlord class, between the proletariat and the bourgeoisie, and between the peasantry and urban petty bourgeoisie on the one hand and the bourgeoisie on the other—still remained, but that they had all been relegated to a secondary or subordinate position as a result of the war of aggression unleashed by Japan; and that throughout China opposition to Japanese imperialism had become the common demand of the people of all classes and strata, except for a handful of pro-Japanese traitors among the big landlords and the big bourgeoisie.

As the contradiction between China and Japan ascended and became the principal one, the contradiction between China and imperialist countries such as Britain and the United States descended to a secondary or subordinate position. The rift between Japan and the other imperialist countries had widened as a result of Japanese imperialism's attempt to turn China into its own exclusive colony. This rendered it possible for China to make use of these contradictions to isolate and oppose Japanese imperialism.

In the face of Japanese imperialist aggression, was the

2. The Victory of People's War

Party to continue with the civil war and the Agrarian Revolution? Or was it to hold aloft the banner of national liberation, unite with all the forces that could be united to form a broad national united front and concentrate on fighting the Japanese aggressors? This was the problem sharply confronting our Party.

The Communist Party of China and Comrade Mao Tse-tung formulated the line of the Anti-Japanese National United Front on the basis of their analysis of the new situation. Holding aloft the banner of national liberation, our Party issued the call for national unity and united resistance to Japanese imperialism, a call which won fervent support from the people of the whole country. Thanks to the common efforts of our Party and of China's patriotic armies and people, the Kuomintang ruling clique was eventually compelled to stop the civil war, and a new situation with Kuomintang-Communist cooperation for joint resistance to Japan was brought about.

In the summer of 1937 Japanese imperialism unleashed its all-out war of aggression against China. The nation-wide War of Resistance thus broke out.

Could the War of Resistance be victorious? And how was victory to be won? These were the questions to which all the Chinese people demanded immediate answers.

The defeatists came forward with the assertion that China was no match for Japan and that the nation was bound to be subjugated. The blind optimists came forward with the assertion that China could win very quickly, without much effort.

Basing himself on a concrete analysis of the Chinese nation and of Japanese imperialism—the two aspects of the principal contradiction—Comrade Mao Tse-tung showed that while the "theory of national subjugation" was

2. The Victory of People's War

wrong, the "theory of quick victory" was untenable, and he concluded that the War of Resistance would be a protracted one in which China would finally be victorious.

In his celebrated work *On Protracted War*, Comrade Mao Tse-tung pointed out the contrasting features of China and Japan, the two sides in the war. Japan was a powerful imperialist country. But Japanese imperialism was in its era of decline and doom. The war it had unleashed was a war of aggression, a war that was retrogressive and barbarous; it was deficient in manpower and material resources and could not stand a protracted war; it was engaged in an unjust cause and therefore had meagre support internationally. China, on the other hand, was a weak semi-colonial and semi-feudal country. But she was in her era of progress. She was fighting a war against aggression, a war that was progressive and just; she had sufficient manpower and material resources to sustain a protracted war; internationally, China enjoyed extensive sympathy and support. These comprised all the basic factors in the Sino-Japanese war.

He went on to show how these factors would influence the course of the war. Japan's advantage was temporary and would gradually diminish as a result of our efforts. Her disadvantages were fundamental: they could not be overcome and would gradually grow in the course of the war. China's disadvantage was temporary and could be gradually overcome. China's advantages were fundamental and would play an increasingly positive role in the course of the war. Japan's advantage and China's disadvantage determined the impossibility of quick victory for China. China's advantages and Japan's disadvantages determined the inevitability of Japan's defeat and China's ultimate victory.

2. *The Victory of People's War*

On the basis of this analysis Comrade Mao Tse-tung formulated the strategy for a protracted war. China's War of Resistance would be protracted, and prolonged efforts would be needed gradually to weaken the enemy's forces and expand our own, so that the enemy would change from being strong to being weak and we would change from being weak to being strong and accumulate sufficient strength finally to defeat him. Comrade Mao Tse-tung pointed out that with the change in the balance of forces between the enemy and ourselves the War of Resistance would pass through three stages, namely, the strategic defensive, the strategic stalemate and the strategic offensive. The protracted war was also a process of mobilizing, organizing and arming the people. It was only by mobilizing the entire people to fight a people's war that the War of Resistance could be persevered in and the Japanese aggressors defeated.

In order to turn the anti-Japanese war into a genuine people's war, our Party firmly relied on the broadest masses of the people, united with all the anti-Japanese forces that could be united, and consolidated and expanded the Anti-Japanese National United Front. The basic line of our Party was: boldly to arouse the masses of the people and expand the people's forces so that, under the leadership of the Party, they could defeat the aggressors and build a new China.

The War of Resistance Against Japan constituted a historical stage in China's new-democratic revolution. The line of our Party during the War of Resistance aimed not only at winning victory in the war, but also at laying the foundations for the nation-wide victory of the new-democratic revolution. Only the accomplishment of the new-democratic revolution makes it possible to carry out a so-

2. The Victory of People's War

cialist revolution. With respect to the relations between the democratic and the socialist revolutions, Comrade Mao Tse-tung said:

> In the writing of an article the second half can be written only after the first half is finished. Resolute leadership of the democratic revolution is the prerequisite for the victory of socialism.[2]

The concrete analysis of concrete conditions and the concrete resolution of concrete contradictions are the living soul of Marxism-Leninism. Comrade Mao Tse-tung has invariably been able to single out the principal contradiction from among a complexity of contradictions, analyze the two aspects of this principal contradiction concretely and, "pressing on irresistibly from this commanding height," successfully solve the problem of understanding and handling the various contradictions.

It was precisely on the basis of such scientific analysis that Comrade Mao Tse-tung correctly formulated the political and military lines for the people's war during the War of Resistance Against Japan, developed his thought on the establishment of rural base areas and the use of the countryside to encircle the cities and finally capture them, and formulated a whole range of principles and policies, strategy and tactics in the political, military, economic and cultural fields for the carrying out of the people's war. It was this that ensured victory in the War of Resistance and created the conditions for the nation-wide victory of the new-democratic revolution.

[2] Mao Tse-tung, "Win the Masses in Their Millions for the Anti-Japanese National United Front," *Selected Works*, Eng. ed., Foreign Languages Press, Peking, 1965, Vol. I, p. 290.

2. The Victory of People's War

In order to win a people's war, it is imperative to build the broadest possible united front and formulate a series of policies which will ensure the fullest mobilization of the basic masses as well as the unity of all the forces that can be united.

The Anti-Japanese National United Front embraced all the anti-Japanese classes and strata. These classes and strata shared a common interest in fighting Japan, an interest which formed the basis of their unity. But they differed in the degree of their firmness in resisting Japan, and there were class contradictions and conflicts of interest among them. Hence the inevitable class struggle within the united front.

In formulating the Party's line of the Anti-Japanese National United Front, Comrade Mao Tse-tung made the following class analysis of Chinese society:

The workers, the peasants and the urban petty bourgeoisie firmly demanded that the War of Resistance should be carried through to the end; they were the main force in the fight against Japanese aggression and constituted the basic masses who demanded unity and progress.

The bourgeoisie was divided into the national and the comprador bourgeoisie. The national bourgeoisie formed the majority of the bourgeoisie; it was rather flabby, often vacillated and had contradictions with the workers, but it also had a certain degree of readiness to oppose imperialism and was one of our allies in the War of Resistance. The comprador bourgeoisie was the bureaucrat-capitalist class, which was very small in number but occupied the ruling position in China. Its members attached themselves to different imperialist powers, some of them being pro-

2. *The Victory of People's War*

Japanese and others pro-British and pro-American. The pro-Japanese section of the comprador bourgeoisie were the capitulators, the overt and covert traitors. The pro-British and pro-American section of this class favored resistance to Japan to a certain extent, but they were not firm in their resistance and very much wished to compromise with Japan, and by their nature they were opposed to the Communist Party and the people.

The landlords fell into different categories; there were the big, the middle and the small landlords. Some of the big landlords became traitors, while others favored resistance but vacillated a great deal. Many of the middle and small landlords had the desire to resist, but there were contradictions between them and the peasants.

In the face of these complicated class relationships, our Party's policy regarding work within the united front was one of both alliance and struggle. That is to say, its policy was to unite with all the anti-Japanese classes and strata, try to win over even those who could be only vacillating and temporary allies, and adopt appropriate policies to adjust the relations among these classes and strata so that they all served the general cause of resisting Japan. At the same time, we had to maintain our Party's principle of independence and initiative, make the bold arousing of the masses and expansion of the people's forces the center of gravity in our work, and wage the necessary struggles against all activities harmful to resistance, unity and progress.

Our Party's Anti-Japanese National United Front policy was different both from Chen Tu-hsiu's Right opportunist policy of all alliance and no struggle, and from Wang Ming's "Left" opportunist policy of all struggle and no alliance. Our Party summed up the lessons of the Right

2. The Victory of People's War

and "Left" opportunist errors and formulated the policy of both alliance and struggle.

Our Party made a series of adjustments in its policies in order to unite all the anti-Japanese parties and groups, including the Kuomintang, and all the anti-Japanese strata in a joint fight against the foe. We pledged ourselves to fight for the complete realization of Dr. Sun Yat-sen's revolutionary Three People's Principles. The government of the Shensi-Kansu-Ningsia revolutionary base area was renamed the Government of the Shensi-Kansu-Ningsia Special Region of the Republic of China. Our Workers' and Peasants' Red Army was redesignated the Eighth Route Army and the New Fourth Army of the National Revolutionary Army. Our land policy, the policy of confiscating the land of the landlords, was changed to one of reducing rent and interest. In our own base areas we carried out the "three-thirds system"[3] in our organs of political power, drawing in those representatives of the petty bourgeoisie, the national bourgeoisie and the enlightened gentry and those members of the Kuomintang who stood for resistance to Japan and did not oppose the Communist Party. In accordance with the principles of the Anti-Japanese National United Front, we also made necessary and appropriate changes in our policies relating to the economy, taxation, labor and wages, anti-espionage, people's rights, culture and education, etc.

While making these policy adjustments, we maintained the independence of the Communist Party, the people's

[3] The "three thirds system" refers to the organs of the political power which were established according to the principle of the Anti-Japanese National United Front and in which the members of the Communist Party, non-Party progressives and the middle elements each occupied one-third of the places.

army and the base areas. We also insisted that the Kuomintang should institute a general mobilization, reform the government apparatus, introduce democracy, improve the people's livelihood, arm the people, and carry out a total war of resistance. We waged a resolute struggle against the Kuomintang's passive resistance to Japan and active opposition to the Communist Party, against its suppression of the people's resistance movement and its treacherous activities for compromise and capitulation.

Past experience had taught us that "Left" errors were liable to crop up after our Party had corrected Right errors, and that Right errors were liable to crop up after it had corrected "Left" errors. "Left" errors were liable to occur when we broke with the Kuomintang ruling clique, and Right errors were liable to occur when we united with it.

After the overcoming of "Left" opportunism and the formation of the Anti-Japanese National United Front, the main danger in our Party was Right opportunism or capitulationism.

Wang Ming, the exponent of "Left" opportunism during the Second Revolutionary Civil War, went to the other extreme in the early days of the War of Resistance Against Japan and became the exponent of Right opportunism, *i.e.*, capitulationism. He countered Comrade Mao Tse-tung's correct line and policies with an out-and-out capitulationist line of his own and a series of ultra-Right policies. He voluntarily abandoned proletarian leadership in the Anti-Japanese National United Front and willingly handed leadership to the Kuomintang. By his advocacy of "everything through the united front" or "everything to be submitted to the united front," he was in effect advocating that everything should go through or be submitted to

2. The Victory of People's War

Chiang Kai-shek and the Kuomintang. He opposed the bold mobilization of the masses, the carrying out of democratic reforms and the improvement of the livelihood of the workers and peasants, and wanted to undermine the worker-peasant alliance which was the foundation of the united front. He did not want the Communist-led base areas of the people's revolutionary forces but wanted to cut off the people's revolutionary forces from their roots. He rejected a people's army led by the Communist Party and wanted to hand over the people's armed forces to Chiang Kai-shek, which would have meant handing over everything the people had. He did not want the leadership of the Party and advocated an alliance between the youth of the Kuomintang and that of the Communist Party to suit Chiang Kai-shek's design of corroding the Communist Party. He decked himself out and presented himself to Chiang Kai-shek, hoping to be given some official appointment. All this was revisionism, pure and simple. If we had acted on Wang Ming's revisionist line and his set of policies, the Chinese people would have been unable to win the War of Resistance Against Japan, still less the subsequent nation-wide victory.

For a time during the War of Resistance, Wang Ming's revisionist line caused harm to the Chinese people's revolutionary cause. But the leading role of Comrade Mao Tse-tung had already been established in the Central Committee of our Party. Under his leadership, all the Marxist-Leninists in the Party carried out a resolute struggle against Wang Ming's errors and rectified them in time. It was this struggle that prevented Wang Ming's erroneous line from doing greater and more lasting damage to the cause of the Party.

Chiang Kai-shek, our teacher by negative example,

2. The Victory of People's War

helped us to correct Wang Ming's mistakes. He repeatedly lectured us with cannons and machine-guns. The gravest lesson was the Southern Anhwei Incident which took place in January 1941. Because some leaders of the New Fourth Army disobeyed the directives of the Central Committee of the Party and followed Wang Ming's revisionist line, its units in southern Anhwei suffered disastrous losses in the surprise attack launched by Chiang Kai-shek and many heroic revolutionary fighters were slaughtered by the Kuomintang reactionaries. The lessons learned at the cost of blood helped to sober many of our comrades and increase their ability to distinguish the correct from the erroneous line.

Comrade Mao Tse-tung constantly summed up the experience gained by the whole Party in implementing the line of the Anti-Japanese National United Front and worked out a whole set of policies in good time. They were mainly as follows:

(1) All people favoring resistance (that is, all the anti-Japanese workers, peasants, soldiers, students and intellectuals, and businessmen) were to unite and form the Anti-Japanese National United Front.

(2) Within the united front, our policy was to be one of independence and initiative, i.e., both unity and independence were necessary.

(3) As far as military strategy was concerned, our policy was to be guerrilla warfare waged independently and with the initiative in our own hands, within the framework of a unified strategy; guerrilla warfare was to be basic, but no chance of waging mobile warfare was to be lost when the conditions were favorable.

(4) In the struggle against the anti-Communist diehards headed by Chiang Kai-shek, our policy was to make

use of contradictions, win over the many, oppose the few and destroy our enemies one by one, and to wage struggles on just grounds, to our advantage, and with restraint.

(5) In the Japanese-occupied and Kuomintang areas our policy was, on the one hand, to develop the united front to the greatest possible extent and, on the other, to have selected cadres working underground. With regard to the forms of organization and struggle, our policy was to assign selected cadres to work under cover for a long period, so as to accumulate strength and bide our time.

(6) As regards the alignment of the various classes within the country, our basic policy was to develop the progressive forces, win over the middle forces and isolate the anti-Communist die-hard forces.

(7) As for the anti-Communist die-hards, we followed a revolutionary dual policy of uniting with them, in so far as they were still capable of bringing themselves to resist Japan, and of struggling against and isolating them, in so far as they were determined to oppose the Communist Party.

(8) With respect to the landlords and the bourgeoisie —even the big landlords and big bourgeoisie—it was necessary to analyze each case and draw distinctions. On the basis of these distinctions we were to formulate different policies so as to achieve our aim of uniting with all the forces that could be united.

The line and the various policies of the Anti-Japanese National United Front formulated by Comrade Mao Tsetung stood the test of the War of Resistance and proved to be entirely correct.

History shows that when confronted by ruthless imperialist aggression, a Communist Party must hold aloft the national banner and, using the weapon of the united

2. The Victory of People's War

front, rally around itself the masses and the patriotic and anti-imperialist people who form more than 90 per cent of a country's population, so as to mobilize all positive factors, unite with all the forces that can be united and isolate to the maximum the common enemy of the whole nation. If we abandon the national banner, adopt a line of "closed-doorism" and thus isolate ourselves, it is out of the question to exercise leadership and develop the people's revolutionary cause, and this in reality amounts to helping the enemy and bringing defeat on ourselves.

History shows that within the united front the Communist Party must maintain its ideological, political and organizational independence, adhere to the principle of independence and initiative, and insist on its leading role. Since there are class differences among the various classes in the united front, the Party must have a correct policy in order to develop the progressive forces, win over the middle forces and oppose the die-hard forces. The Party's work must center on developing the progressive forces and expanding the people's revolutionary forces. This is the only way to maintain and strengthen the united front. "If unity is sought through struggle, it will live; if unity is sought through yielding, it will perish."[4] This is the chief experience gained in our struggle against the die-hard forces.

History shows that during the national-democratic revolution there must be two kinds of alliance within this united front, first, the worker-peasant alliance and, second, the alliance of the working people with the bourgeoisie and other non-working people. The worker-peasant alliance is an alliance of the working class with the peasants

[4] Mao Tse-tung, "Current Problems of Tactics in the Anti-Japanese United Front," *Selected Works*, Vol. II.

and all other working people in town and country. It is the foundation of the united front. Whether the working class can gain leadership of the national-democratic revolution depends on whether it can lead the broad masses of the peasants in struggle and rally them around itself. Only when the working class gains leadership of the peasants, and only on the basis of the worker-peasant alliance, is it possible to establish the second alliance, form a broad united front and wage a people's war victoriously. Otherwise, everything that is done is unreliable, like castles in the air or so much empty talk.

RELY ON THE PEASANTS AND ESTABLISH
RURAL BASE AREAS

The peasantry constituted more than 80 per cent of the entire population of semi-colonial and semi-feudal China. They were subjected to threefold oppression and exploitation by imperialism, feudalism and bureaucrat-capitalism, and they were eager for resistance against Japan and for revolution. It was essential to rely mainly on the peasants if the people's war was to be won.

But at the outset not all comrades in our Party saw this point. The history of our Party shows that in the period of the First Revolutionary Civil War, one of the major errors of the Right opportunists, represented by Chen Tu-hsiu, was their failure to recognize the importance of the peasant question and their opposition to arousing and arming the peasants. In the period of the Second Revolutionary Civil War, one of the major errors of the "Left" opportunists, represented by Wang Ming, was likewise their failure to recognize the importance of the peasant question. They did not realize that it was essential to undertake long-term and painstaking work among the peasants

2. *The Victory of People's War*

and establish revolutionary base areas in the countryside; they were under the illusion that they could rapidly seize the big cities and quickly win nation-wide victory in the revolution. The errors of both the Right and the "Left" opportunists brought serious setbacks and defeats to the Chinese revolution.

As far back as the period of the First Revolutionary Civil War, Comrade Mao Tse-tung had pointed out that the peasant question occupied an extremely important position in the Chinese revolution, that the bourgeois-democratic revolution against imperialism and feudalism was in essence a peasant revolution and that the basic task of the Chinese proletariat in the bourgeois-democratic revolution was to give leadership to the peasants' struggle.

In the period of the War of Resistance Against Japan, Comrade Mao Tse-tung again stressed that the peasants were the most reliable and the most numerous ally of the proletariat and constituted the main force in the War of Resistance. The peasants were the main source of manpower for China's armies. The funds and the supplies needed for a protracted war came chiefly from the peasants. In the anti-Japanese war it was imperative to rely mainly on the peasants and to arouse them to participate in the war on the broadest scale.

The War of Resistance Against Japan was in essence a peasant revolutionary war led by our Party. By arousing and organizing the peasant masses and integrating them with the proletariat, our Party created a powerful force capable of defeating the strongest enemy.

To rely on the peasants, build rural base areas and use the countryside to encircle and finally capture the cities— such was the way to victory in the Chinese revolution.

Basing himself on the characteristics of the Chinese rev-

2. *The Victory of People's War*

olution, Comrade Mao Tse-tung pointed out the importance of building rural revolutionary base areas.

> Since China's key cities have long been occupied by
> the powerful imperialists and their reactionary Chinese
> allies, it is imperative for the revolutionary ranks to turn
> the backward villages into advanced, consolidated base
> areas, into great military, political, economic and cul-
> tural bastions of the revolution from which to fight their
> vicious enemies who are using the cities for attacks on
> the rural districts, and in this way gradually to achieve
> the complete victory of the revolution through pro-
> tracted fighting; it is imperative for them to do so if
> they do not wish to compromise with imperialism and
> its lackeys but are determined to fight on, and if they
> intend to build up and temper their forces, and avoid
> decisive battles with a powerful enemy while their own
> strength is inadequate.[5]

Experience in the period of the Second Revolutionary
Civil War showed that, when this strategic concept of
Comrade Mao Tse-tung's was applied, there was an im-
mense growth in the revolutionary forces and one Red
base area after another was built. Conversely, when it was
violated and the nonsense of the "Left" opportunists was
applied, the revolutionary forces suffered severe damage,
with losses of nearly 100 per cent in the cities and 90 per
cent in the rural areas.

During the War of Resistance Against Japan, the Japanese imperialist forces occupied many of China's big cities
and the main lines of communication, but owing to the
shortage of troops they were unable to occupy the vast

[5] Mao Tse-tung, "The Chinese Revolution and the Chinese Communist Party," *Selected Works,* Vol. II.

2. The Victory of People's War

countryside, which remained the vulnerable sector of the enemy's rule. Consequently, the possibility of building rural base areas became even greater. Shortly after the beginning of the War of Resistance, when the Japanese forces surged into China's hinterland and the Kuomintang forces crumbled and fled in one defeat after another, the Eighth Route and New Fourth Armies led by our Party followed the wise policy laid down by Comrade Mao Tsetung and boldly drove into the areas behind the enemy lines in small contingents and established base areas throughout the countryside. During the eight years of the war, we established nineteen anti-Japanese base areas in northern, central and southern China. With the exception of the big cities and the main lines of communication, the vast territory in the enemy's rear was in the hands of the people.

In the anti-Japanese base areas, we carried out democratic reforms, improved the livelihood of the people, and mobilized and organized the peasant masses. Organs of anti-Japanese democratic political power were established on an extensive scale and the masses of the people enjoyed the democratic right to run their own affairs; at the same time we carried out the policies of "a reasonable burden" and "the reduction of rent and interest," which weakened the feudal system of exploitation and improved the people's livelihood. As a result, the enthusiasm of the peasant masses was deeply aroused, while the various anti-Japanese strata were given due consideration and were thus united. In formulating our policies for the base areas, we also took care that these policies should facilitate our work in the enemy-occupied areas.

In the enemy-occupied cities and villages, we combined legal with illegal struggle, united the basic masses and all

2. The Victory of People's War

patriots, and divided and disintegrated the political power of the enemy and his puppets so as to prepare ourselves to attack the enemy from within in coordination with operations from without when conditions were ripe.

The base areas established by our Party became the center of gravity in the Chinese people's struggle to resist Japan and save the country. Relying on these bases, our Party expanded and strengthened the people's revolutionary forces, persevered in the protracted war and eventually won the War of Resistance Against Japan.

Naturally, it was impossible for the development of the revolutionary base areas to be plain sailing all the time. They constituted a tremendous threat to the enemy and were bound to be attacked. Therefore, their development was a tortuous process of expansion, contraction and then renewed expansion. Between 1937 and 1940 the population in the anti-Japanese base areas grew to 100,000,000. But in 1941-42 the Japanese imperialists used the major part of their invading forces to launch frantic attacks on our base areas and to wreak havoc. Meanwhile, the Kuomintang, too, encircled these base areas, blockaded them and went so far as to attack them. So by 1942, the anti-Japanese base areas had contracted and their population was down to less than 50,000,000. Placing complete reliance on the masses, our Party resolutely adopted a series of correct policies and measures, with the result that the base areas were able to hold out under extremely difficult circumstances. After this setback, the army and the people in the base areas were tempered, and grew stronger. From 1943 onwards, our base areas were gradually restored and expanded, and by 1945 the population had grown to 160,000,000. Taking the entire course of the Chinese revolution into account, our revolutionary base areas went

2. The Victory of People's War

through even more ups and downs, and they weathered a great many tests before the small, separate base areas, expanding in a series of waves, gradually developed into extensive and contiguous base areas.

At the same time, the work of building the revolutionary base areas was a grand rehearsal in preparation for nation-wide victory. In these base areas, we built the Party, ran the organs of state power, built the people's armed forces and set up mass organizations; we engaged in industry and agriculture and operated cultural, educational and all other undertakings necessary for the independent existence of a separate region. Our base areas were in fact a state in miniature. And with the steady expansion of our work in the base areas, our Party established a powerful people's army, trained cadres for various kinds of work, accumulated experience in many fields and built up both the material and the moral strength that provided favorable conditions for nation-wide victory.

The revolutionary base areas established in the War of Resistance later became the spring-boards for the People's War of Liberation, in which the Chinese people defeated the Kuomintang reactionaries. In the War of Liberation we continued the policy of first encircling the cities from the countryside and then capturing the cities, and thus won nation-wide victory.

BUILD A PEOPLE'S ARMY OF A NEW TYPE

"Without a people's army the people have nothing."[6] This is the conclusion drawn by Comrade Mao Tse-tung from the Chinese people's experience in their long years

[6] Mao Tse-tung, "On Coalition Government," *Selected Works*, Vol. III.

2. The Victory of People's War

of revolutionary struggle, experience that was bought in blood. This is a universal truth of Marxism-Leninism.

The special feature of the Chinese revolution was armed revolution against armed counter-revolution. The main form of struggle was war and the main form of organization was the army which was under the absolute leadership of the Chinese Communist Party, while all the other forms of organization and struggle led by our Party were coordinated, directly or indirectly, with the war.

During the First Revolutionary Civil War, many fine Party comrades took an active part in the armed revolutionary struggle. But our Party was then still in its infancy and did not have a clear understanding of this special feature of the Chinese revolution. It was only after the First Revolutionary Civil War, only after the Kuomintang had betrayed the revolution, massacred large numbers of Communists and destroyed all the revolutionary mass organizations, that our Party reached a clearer understanding of the supreme importance of organizing revolutionary armed forces and of studying the strategy and tactics of revolutionary war, and created the Workers' and Peasants' Red Army, the first people's army under the leadership of the Communist Party of China.

During the Second Revolutionary Civil War, the Workers' and Peasants' Red Army created by Comrade Mao Tse-tung grew considerably and at one time reached a total of 300,000 men. But it later lost nine-tenths of its forces as a result of the wrong political and military lines followed by the "Left" opportunist leadership.

At the start of the War of Resistance Against Japan, the people's army led by the Chinese Communist Party had only a little over 40,000 men. The Kuomintang reactionaries attempted to restrict, weaken and destroy this peo-

2. *The Victory of People's War*

ple's army in every conceivable way. Comrade Mao Tse-tung pointed out that, in these circumstances, in order to sustain the War of Resistance and defeat the Japanese aggressors, it was imperative greatly to expand and consolidate the Eighth Route and New Fourth Armies and all the guerrilla units led by our Party. The whole Party should give close attention to war and study military affairs. Every Party member should be ready at all times to take up arms and go to the front.

Comrade Mao Tse-tung also incisively stated that Communists do not fight for personal military power but must fight for military power for the Party and for the people.

Guided by the Party's correct line of expanding the revolutionary armed forces, the Communist-led Eighth Route and New Fourth Armies and anti-Japanese guerrilla units promptly went to the forefront at the very beginning of the war. We spread the seeds of the people's armed forces in the vast areas behind the enemy lines and kindled the flames of guerrilla warfare everywhere. Our people's army steadily expanded in the struggle, so that by the end of the war it was already a million strong, and there was also a militia of over two million. That was why we were able to engage nearly two-thirds of the Japanese forces of aggression and 95 per cent of the puppet troops and to become the main force in the War of Resistance Against Japan. While resisting the Japanese invading forces, we repulsed three large-scale anti-Communist onslaughts launched by the Kuomintang reactionaries in 1939, 1941 and 1943, and smashed their countless "friction-mongering" activities.

Why were the Eighth Route and New Fourth Armies able to grow big and strong from being small and weak

2. The Victory of People's War

and to score such great victories in the War of Resistance Against Japan?

The fundamental reason was that the Eighth Route and New Fourth Armies were founded on Comrade Mao Tse-tung's theory of army building. They were armies of a new type, a people's army, which wholeheartedly serves the interests of the people.

Guided by Comrade Mao Tse-tung's theory on building a people's army, our army was under the absolute leadership of the Chinese Communist Party and most loyally carried out the Party's Marxist-Leninist line and policies. It had a high degree of conscious discipline and was heroically inspired to destroy all enemies and conquer all difficulties. Internally there was full unity between cadres and fighters, between those in higher and those in lower positions of responsibility, between the different departments and between the various fraternal army units. Externally, there was similarly full unity between the army and the people and between the army and the local government.

During the anti-Japanese war our army staunchly performed the three tasks set by Comrade Mao Tse-tung, namely, fighting, mass work, and production, and it was at the same time a fighting force, a political work force and a production corps. Everywhere it went, it did propaganda work among the masses, organized and armed them and helped them set up revolutionary political power. Our armymen strictly observed the Three Main Rules of Discipline and the Eight Points for Attention,[7] carried

[7] The Three Main Rules of Discipline and the Eight Points for Attention were drawn up by Comrade Mao Tse-tung for the Chinese Workers' and Peasants' Red Army during the Agrarian Revolutionary War and were later adopted as rules of discipline by the Eighth Route Army and the New Fourth Army and the present

2. The Victory of People's War

out campaigns to "support the government and cherish the people," and did good deeds for the people everywhere. They also made use of every possibility to engage in production themselves so as to overcome economic difficulties, better their own livelihood and lighten the people's burden. By their exemplary conduct they won the whole-hearted support of the masses, who affectionately called them "our own boys."

Our army consisted of local forces as well as of regular forces; moreover, it energetically built and developed the militia, thus practising the system of combining the three military formations, *i.e.*, the regular forces, the local forces and the militia.

Our army also pursued correct policies in winning over enemy officers and men and in giving lenient treatment to prisoners of war. During the anti-Japanese war we not only brought about the revolt and surrender of large num-

---

People's Liberation Army. As these rules varied slightly in content in the army units of different areas, the General Headquarters of the Chinese People's Liberation Army in October 1947 issued a standard version as follows:

The Three Main Rules of Discipline:

(1) Obey orders in all your actions.
(2) Do not take a single needle or piece of thread from the masses.
(3) Turn in everything captured.

The Eight Points for Attention:

(1) Speak politely.
(2) Pay fairly for what you buy.
(3) Return everything you borrow.
(4) Pay for anything you damage.
(5) Do not hit or swear at people.
(6) Do not damage crops.
(7) Do not take liberties with women.
(8) Do not ill-treat captives.

bers of puppet troops, but succeeded in converting not a few Japanese prisoners, who had been badly poisoned by fascist ideology. After they were politically awakened, they organized themselves into anti-war organizations such as the League for the Liberation of the Japanese People, the Anti-War League of the Japanese in China and the League of Awakened Japanese, helped us to disintegrate the Japanese army and cooperated with us in opposing Japanese militarism. Comrade Sanzo Nosaka, the leader of the Japanese Communist Party, who was then in Yenan, gave us great help in this work.

The essence of Comrade Mao Tse-tung's theory of army building is that in building a people's army prominence must be given to politics, *i.e.*, the army must first and foremost be built on a political basis. Politics is the commander, politics is the soul of everything. Political work is the lifeline of our army. True, a people's army must pay attention to the constant improvement of its weapons and equipment and its military technique, but in its fighting it does not rely purely on weapons and technique, it relies mainly on politics, on the proletarian revolutionary consciousness and courage of the commanders and fighters, on the support and backing of the masses.

Owing to the application of Comrade Mao Tse-tung's line on army building, there has prevailed in our army at all times a high level of proletarian political consciousness, an atmosphere of keenness to study the thought of Mao Tse-tung, an excellent morale, a solid unity and a deep hatred for the enemy, and thus a gigantic moral force has been brought into being. In battle it has feared neither hardships nor death, it has been able to charge or hold its ground as the conditions require. One man can play the role of several, dozens or even hundreds, and miracles can be performed.

All this makes the people's army led by the Chinese Communist Party fundamentally different from any bourgeois army, and from all the armies of the old type which served the exploiting classes and were driven and utilized by a handful of people. The experience of the people's war in China shows that a people's army created in accordance with Comrade Mao Tse-tung's theory of army building is incomparably strong and invincible.

CARRY OUT THE STRATEGY AND TACTICS OF PEOPLE'S WAR

Engels said, "The emancipation of the proletariat, in its turn, will have its specific expression in military affairs and create its specific, new military method."[8] Engels' profound prediction has been fulfilled in the revolutionary wars waged by the Chinese people under the leadership of the Chinese Communist Party. In the course of protracted armed struggle, we have created a whole range of strategy and tactics of people's war by which we have been able to utilize our strong points to attack the enemy at his weak points.

During the War of Resistance Against Japan, on the basis of his comprehensive analysis of the enemy and ourselves, Comrade Mao Tse-tung laid down the following strategic principle for the Communist-led Eighth Route and New Fourth Armies: "Guerrilla warfare is basic, but lose no chance for mobile warfare under favorable condi-

[8] Frederick Engels, "Possibilities and Perspectives of the War of the Holy Alliance Against France in 1852," *Collected Works of Marx and Engels*, Russ. ed., Moscow, 1956, Vol. VII, p. 509.

2. *The Victory of People's War*

tions."[9] He raised guerrilla warfare to the level of strategy, because, if they are to defeat a formidable enemy, revolutionary armed forces should not fight with a reckless disregard for the consequences when there is a great disparity between their own strength and the enemy's. If they do, they will suffer serious losses and bring heavy setbacks to the revolution. Guerrilla warfare is the only way to mobilize and apply the whole strength of the people against the enemy, the only way to expand our forces in the course of the war, deplete and weaken the enemy, gradually change the balance of forces between the enemy and ourselves, switch from guerrilla to mobile warfare, and finally defeat the enemy.

In the initial period of the Second Revolutionary Civil War, Comrade Mao Tse-tung enumerated the basic tactics of guerrilla warfare as follows: "The enemy advances, we retreat; the enemy camps, we harass; the enemy tires, we attack; the enemy retreats, we pursue."[10] Guerrilla war tactics were further developed during the War of Resistance Against Japan. In the base areas behind the enemy lines, everybody joined in the fighting—the troops and the civilian population, men and women, old and young; every single village fought. Various ingenious methods of fighting were devised, including "sparrow warfare,"[11]

[9] Mao Tse-tung, "On Protracted War," *Selected Works*, Vol. II.
[10] Mao Tse-tung, "A Single Spark Can Start a Prairie Fire," *Selected Works*, Eng. ed., FLP, Peking, 1965, Vol. I, p. 124.

[11] Sparrow warfare is a popular method of fighting created by the Communist-led anti-Japanese guerrilla units and militia behind the enemy lines. It was called sparrow warfare because, first, it was used diffusely, like the flight of sparrows in the sky; and because, second, it was used flexibly by guerrillas or militiamen, operating in threes or fives, appearing and disappearing unexpectedly and wounding, killing, depleting and wearing out the enemy forces.

2. The Victory of People's War

land-mine warfare, tunnel warfare, sabotage warfare, and guerrilla warfare on lakes and rivers.

In the later period of the War of Resistance Against Japan and during the Third Revolutionary Civil War, we switched our strategy from that of guerrilla warfare as the primary form of fighting to that of mobile warfare in the light of the changes in the balance of forces between the enemy and ourselves. By the middle, and especially the later, period of the Third Revolutionary Civil War, our operations had developed into large-scale mobile warfare, including the storming of big cities.

War of annihilation is the fundamental guiding principle of our military operations. This guiding principle should be put into effect regardless of whether mobile or guerrilla warfare is the primary form of fighting. It is true that in guerrilla warfare much should be done to disrupt and harass the enemy, but it is still necessary actively to advocate and fight battles of annihilation whenever conditions are favorable. In mobile warfare superior forces must be concentrated in every battle so that the enemy forces can be wiped out one by one. Comrade Mao Tse-tung has pointed out:

> A battle in which the enemy is routed is not basically decisive in a contest with a foe of great strength. A battle of annihilation, on the other hand, produces a great and immediate impact on any enemy. Injuring all of a man's ten fingers is not as effective as chopping off one, and routing ten enemy divisions is not as effective as annihilating one of them.[12]

Battles of annihilation are the most effective way of hitting

[12] Mao Tse-tung, "Problems of Strategy in China's Revolutionary War," *Selected Works*, Eng. ed., FLP, Peking, 1965, Vol. I, p. 248.

2. The Victory of People's War

the enemy; each time one of his brigades or regiments is wiped out, he will have one brigade or one regiment less, and the enemy forces will be demoralized and will disintegrate. By fighting battles of annihilation, our army is able to take prisoners of war or capture weapons from the enemy in every battle, and the morale of our army rises, our army units get bigger, our weapons become better, and our combat effectiveness continually increases.

In his celebrated ten cardinal military principles Comrade Mao Tse-tung pointed out:

In every battle, concentrate an absolutely superior force (two, three, four and sometimes even five or six times the enemy's strength), encircle the enemy forces completely, strive to wipe them out thoroughly and do not let any escape from the net. In special circumstances, use the method of dealing crushing blows to the enemy, that is, concentrate all our strength to make a frontal attack and also to attack one or both of his flanks, with the aim of wiping out one part and routing another so that our army can swiftly move its troops to smash other enemy forces. Strive to avoid battles of attrition in which we lose more than we gain or only break even. In this way, although we are inferior as a whole (in terms of numbers), we are absolutely superior in every part and every specific campaign, and this ensures victory in the campaign. As time goes on, we shall become superior as a whole and eventually wipe out all the enemy.[13]

At the same time, he said that we should first attack dispersed or isolated enemy forces and only attack concentrated and strong enemy forces later; that we should strive

[13] Mao Tse-tung, "The Present Situation and Our Tasks," *Selected Works,* Eng. ed., FLP, Peking, 1961, Vol. IV, p. 161.

to wipe out the enemy through mobile warfare; that we should fight no battle unprepared and fight no battle we are not sure of winning; and that in any battle we fight we should develop our army's strong points and its excellent style of fighting. These are the major principles of fighting a war of annihilation.

In order to annihilate the enemy, we must adopt the policy of luring him in deep and abandon some cities and districts of our own accord in a planned way, so as to let him in. It is only after letting the enemy in that the people can take part in the war in various ways and that the power of a people's war can be fully exerted. It is only after letting the enemy in that he can be compelled to divide up his forces, take on heavy burdens and commit mistakes. In other words, we must let the enemy become elated, stretch out all his ten fingers and become hopelessly bogged down. Thus, we can concentrate superior forces to destroy the enemy forces one by one, to eat them up mouthful by mouthful. Only by wiping out the enemy's effective strength can cities and localities be finally held or seized. We are firmly against dividing up our forces to defend all positions and putting up resistance at every place for fear that our territory might be lost and our pots and pans smashed, since this can neither wipe out the enemy forces nor hold cities or localities.

Comrade Mao Tse-tung has provided a masterly summary of the strategy and tactics of people's war: You fight in your way and we fight in ours; we fight when we can win and move away when we can't.

In other words, you rely on modern weapons and we rely on highly conscious revolutionary people; you give full play to your superiority and we give full play to ours; you have your way of fighting and we have ours. When

2. The Victory of People's War

you want to fight us, we don't let you and you can't even find us. But when we want to fight you, we make sure that you can't get away and we hit you squarely on the chin and wipe you out. When we are able to wipe you out, we do so with a vengeance; when we can't, we see to it that you don't wipe us out. It is opportunism if one won't fight when one can win. It is adventurism if one insists on fighting when one can't win. Fighting is the pivot of all our strategy and tactics. It is because of the necessity of fighting that we admit the necessity of moving away. The sole purpose of moving away is to fight and bring about the final and complete destruction of the enemy. This strategy and these tactics can be applied only when one relies on the broad masses of the people, and such application brings the superiority of people's war into full play. However superior he may be in technical equipment and whatever tricks he may resort to, the enemy will find himself in the passive position of having to receive blows, and the initiative will always be in our hands.

We grew from a small and weak to a large and strong force and finally defeated formidable enemies at home and abroad because we carried out the strategy and tactics of people's war. During the eight years of the War of Resistance Against Japan, the people's army led by the Chinese Communist Party fought more than 125,000 engagements with the enemy and put out of action more than 1,700,000 Japanese and puppet troops. In the three years of the War of Liberation, we put eight million of the Kuomintang's reactionary troops out of action and won the great victory of the people's revolution.

ADHERE TO THE POLICY OF SELF-RELIANCE

The Chinese people's War of Resistance Against Japan

2. The Victory of People's War

was an important part of the Anti-Fascist World War. The victory of the Anti-Fascist War as a whole was the result of the common struggle of the people of the world. By its participation in the war against Japan at the final stage, the Soviet army under the leadership of the Communist Party of the Soviet Union headed by Stalin played a significant part in bringing about the defeat of Japanese imperialism. Great contributions were made by the peoples of Korea, Viet Nam, Mongolia, Laos, Cambodia, Indonesia, Burma, India, Pakistan, Malaya, the Philippines, Thailand and certain other Asian countries. The people of the Americas, Oceania, Europe and Africa also made their contribution.

Under extremely difficult circumstances, the Communist Party of Japan and the revolutionary forces of the Japanese people kept up their valiant and staunch struggle, and played their part in the defeat of Japanese fascism.

The common victory was won by all the peoples, who gave one another support and encouragement. Yet each country was, above all, liberated as a result of its own people's efforts.

The Chinese people enjoyed the support of other peoples in winning both the War of Resistance Against Japan and the People's Liberation War, and yet victory was mainly the result of the Chinese people's own efforts. Certain people assert that China's victory in the War of Resistance was due entirely to foreign assistance. This absurd assertion is in tune with that of the Japanese militarists.

The liberation of the masses is accomplished by the masses themselves—this is a basic principle of Marxism-Leninism. Revolution or people's war in any country is

2. The Victory of People's War

the business of the masses in that country and should be carried out primarily by their own efforts; there is no other way.

During the War of Resistance Against Japan, our Party maintained that China should rely mainly on her own strength while at the same time trying to get as much foreign assistance as possible. We firmly opposed the Kuomintang ruling clique's policy of exclusive reliance on foreign aid. In the eyes of the Kuomintang and Chiang Kai-shek, China's industry and agriculture were no good, her weapons and equipment were no good, nothing in China was any good, so that if she wanted to defeat Japan, she had to depend on other countries, and particularly on the U. S.-British imperialists. This was completely slavish thinking. Our policy was diametrically opposed to that of the Kuomintang. Our Party held that it was possible to exploit the contradictions between U. S.-British imperialism and Japanese imperialism, but that no reliance could be placed on the former. In fact, the U. S.-British imperialists repeatedly plotted to bring about a "Far Eastern Munich" in order to arrive at a compromise with Japanese imperialism at China's expense, and for a considerable period of time they provided the Japanese aggressors with war matériel. In helping China during that period, the U. S. imperialists harbored the sinister design of turning China into a colony of their own.

Comrade Mao Tse-tung said: "China has to rely mainly on her own efforts in the War of Resistance."[14] He added, "We hope for foreign aid but cannot be dependent on it;

[14] Mao Tse-tung, "Interview with Three Correspondents from the Central News Agency, the *Sao Tang Pao* and the *Hsin Min Pao*," *Selected Works*, Vol. II.

2. The Victory of People's War

we depend on our own efforts, on the creative power of the whole army and the entire people."[15]

Self-reliance was especially important for the people's armed forces and the Liberated Areas led by our Party.

The Kuomintang government gave the Eighth Route and New Fourth Armies some small allowances in the initial stage of the anti-Japanese war, but gave them not a single penny later. The Liberated Areas faced great difficulties as a result of the Japanese imperialists' savage attacks and brutal "mopping-up" campaigns, of the Kuomintang's military encirclement and economic blockade and of natural calamities. The difficulties were particularly great in the years 1941 and 1942, when we were very short of food and clothing.

What were we to do? Comrade Mao Tse-tung asked: How has mankind managed to keep alive from time immemorial? Has it not been by men using their hands to provide for themselves? Why should we, their latter-day descendants, be devoid of this tiny bit of wisdom? Why can't we use our own hands?

The Central Committee of the Party and Comrade Mao Tse-tung put forward the policies of "ample food and clothing through self-reliance" and "develop the economy and ensure supplies," and the army and the people of the Liberated Areas accordingly launched an extensive production campaign, with the main emphasis on agriculture.

Difficulties are not invincible monsters. If everyone cooperates and fights them, they will be overcome. The Kuomintang reactionaries thought that it could starve us to death by cutting off allowances and imposing an economic blockade, but in fact it helped us by stimulating us to rely

[15] Mao Tse-tung, "We Must Learn to Do Economic Work," *Selected Works*, Vol. III.

on our own efforts to surmount our difficulties. While launching the great campaign for production, we applied the policy of "better troops and simpler administration" and economized in the use of manpower and material resources; thus we not only surmounted the severe material difficulties and successfully met the crisis, but lightened the people's burden, improved their livelihood and laid the material foundations for victory in the anti-Japanese war.

The problem of military equipment was solved mainly by relying on the capture of arms from the enemy, though we did turn out some weapons too. Chiang Kai-shek, the Japanese imperialists and the U.S. imperialists have all been our "chiefs of transportation corps." The arsenals of the imperialists always provide the oppressed peoples and nations with arms.

The people's armed forces led by our Party independently waged people's war on a large scale and won great victories without any material aid from outside, both during the more than eight years of the anti-Japanese war and during the more than three years of the People's War of Liberation.

Comrade Mao Tse-tung has said that our fundamental policy should rest on the foundation of our own strength. Only by relying on our own efforts can we in all circumstances remain invincible.

The peoples of the world invariably support each other in their struggles against imperialism and its lackeys. Those countries which have won victory are duty bound to support and aid the peoples who have not yet done so. Nevertheless, foreign aid can only play a supplementary role.

In order to make a revolution and to fight a people's war and be victorious, it is imperative to adhere to the

2. The Victory of People's War

policy of self-reliance, rely on the strength of the masses in one's own country and prepare to carry on the fight independently even when all material aid from outside is cut off. If one does not operate by one's own efforts, does not independently ponder and solve the problems of the revolution in one's own country and does not rely on the strength of the masses, but leans wholly on foreign aid —even though this be aid from socialist countries which persist in revolution—no victory can be won, or be consolidated even if it is won.

THE INTERNATIONAL SIGNIFICANCE OF COMRADE MAO TSE-TUNG'S THEORY OF PEOPLE'S WAR

The Chinese revolution is a continuation of the Great October Revolution. The road of the October Revolution is the common road for all people's revolutions. The Chinese revolution and the October Revolution have in common the following basic characteristics: (1) Both were led by the working class with a Marxist-Leninist party as its nucleus. (2) Both were based on the worker-peasant alliance. (3) In both cases state power was seized through violent revolution and the dictatorship of the proletariat was established. (4) In both cases the socialist system was built after victory in the revolution. (5) Both were component parts of the proletarian world revolution.

Naturally, the Chinese revolution had its own peculiar characteristics. The October Revolution took place in imperialist Russia, but the Chinese revolution broke out in a semi-colonial and semi-feudal country. The former was a proletarian socialist revolution, while the latter developed into a socialist revolution after the complete victory of the new-democratic revolution. The October Revolution began with armed uprisings in the cities and then spread to

2. *The Victory of People's War*

the countryside, while the Chinese revolution won nation-wide victory through the encirclement of the cities from the rural areas and the final capture of the cities.

Comrade Mao Tse-tung's great merit lies in the fact that he has succeeded in integrating the universal truth of Marxism-Leninism with the concrete practice of the Chinese revolution and has enriched and developed Marxism-Leninism by his masterly generalization and summation of the experience gained during the Chinese people's protracted revolutionary struggle.

Comrade Mao Tse-tung's theory of people's war has been proved by the long practice of the Chinese revolution to be in accord with the objective laws of such wars and to be invincible. It has not only been valid for China, it is a great contribution to the revolutionary struggles of the oppressed nations and peoples throughout the world.

The people's war led by the Chinese Communist Party, comprising the War of Resistance and the Revolutionary Civil Wars, lasted for twenty-two years. It constitutes the most drawn-out and most complex people's war led by the proletariat in modern history, and it has been the richest in experience.

In the last analysis, the Marxist-Leninist theory of proletarian revolution is the theory of the seizure of state power by revolutionary violence, the theory of countering war against the people by people's war. As Marx so aptly put it, "Force is the midwife of every old society pregnant with a new one."[16]

It was on the basis of the lessons derived from the people's wars in China that Comrade Mao Tse-tung, using the simplest and the most vivid language, advanced the fa-

[16] Karl Marx, *Capital*, Eng. ed., Foreign Languages Publishing House, Moscow, 1954, Vol. I, p. 751.

2. *The Victory of People's War*

mous thesis that "political power grows out of the barrel of a gun."[17]

He clearly pointed out:

> The seizure of power by armed force, the settlement of the issue by war, is the central task and the highest form of revolution. This Marxist-Leninist principle of revolution holds good universally, for China and for all other countries.[18]

War is the product of imperialism and the system of exploitation of man by man. Lenin said that "war is always and everywhere begun by the exploiters themselves, by the ruling and oppressing classes."[19] So long as imperialism and the system of exploitation of man by man exist, the imperialists and reactionaries will invariably rely on armed force to maintain their reactionary rule and impose war on the oppressed nations and peoples. This is an objective law independent of man's will.

In the world today, all the imperialists headed by the United States and their lackeys, without exception, are strengthening their state machinery, and especially their armed forces. U.S. imperialism, in particular, is carrying out armed aggression and suppression everywhere.

What should the oppressed nations and the oppressed people do in the face of wars of aggression and armed suppression by the imperialists and their lackeys? Should they submit and remain slaves in perpetuity? Or should they rise in resistance and fight for their liberation?

[17] Mao Tse-tung, "Problems of War and Strategy," *Selected Works*, Vol. II.

[18] *Ibid.*

[19] V. I. Lenin, "The Revolutionary Army and the Revolutionary Government," *Collected Works*, Eng. ed., FLPH, Moscow, 1962, Vol. VIII, p. 565.

2. The Victory of People's War

Comrade Mao Tse-tung answered this question in vivid terms. He said that after long investigation and study the Chinese people discovered that all the imperialists and their lackeys "have swords in their hands and are out to kill. The people have come to understand this and so act after the same fashion."[20] This is called doing unto them what they do unto us.

In the last analysis, whether one dares to wage a tit-for-tat struggle against armed aggression and suppression by the imperialists and their lackeys, whether one dares to fight a people's war against them, is tantamount to whether one dares to embark on revolution. This is the most effective touchstone for distinguishing genuine from fake revolutionaries and Marxist-Leninists.

In view of the fact that some people were afflicted with the fear of the imperialists and reactionaries, Comrade Mao Tse-tung put forward his famous thesis that "the imperialists and all reactionaries are paper tigers." He said,

> All reactionaries are paper tigers. In appearance, the reactionaries are terrifying, but in reality they are not so powerful. From a long-term point of view, it is not the reactionaries but the people who are really powerful.[21]

The history of people's war in China and other countries provides conclusive evidence that the growth of the people's revolutionary forces from weak and small beginnings into strong and large forces is a universal law of de-

[20] Mao Tse-tung, "The Situation and Our Policy After the Victory in the War of Resistance Against Japan," *Selected Works*, Eng. ed., FLP, Peking, 1961, Vol. IV, pp. 14-15.

[21] Mao Tse-tung, "Talk with the American Correspondent Anna Louise Strong," *Selected Works*, Eng. ed., FLP, Peking, 1961, Vol. IV, p. 100.

2. The Victory of People's War

velopment of class struggle, a universal law of development of people's war. A people's war inevitably meets with many difficulties, with ups and downs and setbacks in the course of its development, but no force can alter its general trend towards inevitable triumph.

Comrade Mao Tse-tung points out that we must despise the enemy strategically and take full account of him tactically.

To despise the enemy strategically is an elementary requirement for a revolutionary. Without the courage to despise the enemy and without daring to win, it will be simply impossible to make revolution and wage a people's war, let alone to achieve victory.

It is also very important for revolutionaries to take full account of the enemy tactically. It is likewise impossible to win victory in a people's war without taking full account of the enemy tactically, and without examining the concrete conditions, without being prudent and giving great attention to the study of the art of struggle, and without adopting appropriate forms of struggle in the concrete practice of the revolution in each country and with regard to each concrete problem of struggle.

Dialectical and historical materialism teaches us that what is important primarily is not that which at the given moment seems to be durable and yet is already beginning to die away, but that which is arising and developing, even though at the given moment it may not appear to be durable, for only that which is arising and developing is invincible.

Why can the apparently weak new-born forces always triumph over the decadent forces which appear so powerful? The reason is that truth is on their side and that the masses are on their side, while the reactionary classes are

2. The Victory of People's War

always divorced from the masses and set themselves against the masses.

This has been borne out by the victory of the Chinese revolution, by the history of all revolutions, the whole history of class struggle and the entire history of mankind.

The imperialists are extremely afraid of Comrade Mao Tse-tung's thesis that "imperialism and all reactionaries are paper tigers," and the revisionists are extremely hostile to it. They all oppose and attack this thesis and the philistines follow suit by ridiculing it. But all this cannot in the least diminish its importance. The light of truth cannot be dimmed by anybody.

Comrade Mao Tse-tung's theory of people's war solves not only the problem of daring to fight a people's war, but also that of how to wage it.

Comrade Mao Tse-tung is a great statesman and military scientist, proficient at directing war in accordance with its laws. By the line and policies, the strategy and tactics he formulated for the people's war, he led the Chinese people in steering the ship of the people's war past all hidden reefs to the shores of victory in most complicated and difficult conditions.

It must be emphasized that Comrade Mao Tse-tung's theory of the establishment of rural revolutionary base areas and the encirclement of the cities from the countryside is of outstanding and universal practical importance for the present revolutionary struggles of all the oppressed nations and peoples, and particularly for the revolutionary struggles of the oppressed nations and peoples in Asia, Africa and Latin America against imperialism and its lackeys.

Many countries and peoples in Asia, Africa and Latin America are now being subjected to aggression and en-

2. The Victory of People's War

slavement on a serious scale by the imperialists headed by the United States and their lackeys. The basic political and economic conditions in many of these countries have many similarities to those that prevailed in old China. As in China, the peasant question is extremely important in these regions. The peasants constitute the main force of the national-democratic revolution against the imperialists and their lackeys. In committing aggression against these countries, the imperialists usually begin by seizing the big cities and the main lines of communication, but they are unable to bring the vast countryside completely under their control. The countryside, and the countryside alone, can provide the broad areas in which the revolutionaries can maneuver freely. The countryside, and the countryside alone, can provide the revolutionary bases from which the revolutionaries can go forward to final victory. Precisely for this reason, Comrade Mao Tse-tung's theory of establishing revolutionary base areas in the rural districts and encircling the cities from the countryside is attracting more and more attention among the people in these regions.

Taking the entire globe, if North America and Western Europe can be called "the cities of the world," then Asia, Africa and Latin America constitute "the rural areas of the world." Since World War II, the proletarian revolutionary movement has for various reasons been temporarily held back in the North American and West European capitalist countries, while the people's revolutionary movement in Asia, Africa and Latin America has been growing vigorously. In a sense, the contemporary world revolution also presents a picture of the encirclement of cities by the rural areas. In the final analysis, the whole cause of world revolution hinges on the revolutionary

2. *The Victory of People's War*

struggles of the Asian, African and Latin American peoples who make up the overwhelming majority of the world's population. The socialist countries should regard it as their internationalist duty to support the people's revolutionary struggles in Asia, Africa and Latin America.

The October Revolution opened up a new era in the revolution of the oppressed nations. The victory of the October Revolution built a bridge between the socialist revolution of the proletariat of the West and the national-democratic revolution of the colonial and semi-colonial countries of the East. The Chinese revolution has successfully solved the problem of how to link up the national-democratic with the socialist revolution in the colonial and semi-colonial countries.

Comrade Mao Tse-tung has pointed out that, in the epoch since the October Revolution, anti-imperialist revolution in any colonial or semi-colonial country is no longer part of the old bourgeois, or capitalist world revolution, but is part of the new world revolution, the proletarian-socialist world revolution.

Comrade Mao Tse-tung has formulated a complete theory of the new-democratic revolution. He indicated that this revolution, which is different from all others, can only be, nay must be, a revolution against imperialism, feudalism and bureaucrat-capitalism waged by the broad masses of the people under the leadership of the proletariat.

This means that the revolution can only be, nay must be, led by the proletariat and the genuinely revolutionary party armed with Marxism-Leninism, and by no other class or party.

This means that the revolution embraces in its ranks not only the workers, peasants and the urban petty bourgeoisie, but also the national bourgeoisie and other patriotic and anti-imperialist democrats.

This means, finally, that the revolution is directed against imperialism, feudalism and bureaucrat-capitalism.

The new-democratic revolution leads to socialism, and not to capitalism.

Comrade Mao Tse-tung's theory of the new-democratic revolution is the Marxist-Leninist theory of revolution by stages as well as the Marxist-Leninist theory of uninterrupted revolution.

Comrade Mao Tse-tung made a correct distinction between the two revolutionary stages, *i.e.*, the national-democratic and the socialist revolutions; at the same time he correctly and closely linked the two. The national-democratic revolution is the necessary preparation for the socialist revolution, and the socialist revolution is the inevitable sequel to the national-democratic revolution. There is no Great Wall between the two revolutionary stages. But the socialist revolution is only possible after the completion of the national-democratic revolution. The more thorough the national-democratic revolution, the better the conditions for the socialist revolution.

The experience of the Chinese revolution shows that the tasks of the national-democratic revolution can be fulfilled only through long and tortuous struggles. In this stage of revolution, imperialism and its lackeys are the principal enemy. In the struggle against imperialism and its lackeys, it is necessary to rally all anti-imperialist patriotic forces, including the national bourgeoisie and all patriotic personages. All those patriotic personages from among the bourgeoisie and other exploiting classes who join the anti-imperialist struggle play a progressive historical role; they are not tolerated by imperialism but welcomed by the proletariat.

It is very harmful to confuse the two stages, that is, the national-democratic and the socialist revolutions. Comrade Mao Tse-tung criticized the wrong idea of "accomplishing both at one stroke," and pointed out that this utopian idea could only weaken the struggle against imperialism and its lackeys, the most urgent task at that time. The Kuomintang reactionaries and the Trotskyites they hired during the War of Resistance deliberately confused these two stages of the Chinese revolution, proclaiming the "theory of a single revolution" and preaching so-called "socialism" without any Communist Party. With this preposterous theory they attempted to swallow up the Communist Party, wipe out any revolution and prevent the advance of the national-democratic revolution, and they used it as a pretext for their non-resistance and capitulation to imperialism. This reactionary theory was buried long ago by the history of the Chinese revolution.

The Khrushchov revisionists are now actively preaching that socialism can be built without the proletariat and without a genuinely revolutionary party armed with the advanced proletarian ideology, and they have cast the fundamental tenets of Marxism-Leninism to the four winds. The revisionists' purpose is solely to divert the oppressed nations from their struggle against imperialism and sabotage their national-democratic revolution, all in the service of imperialism.

The Chinese revolution provides a successful lesson for making a thoroughgoing national-democratic revolution under the leadership of the proletariat; it likewise provides a successful lesson for the timely transition from the national-democratic revolution to the socialist revolution under the leadership of the proletariat.

Mao Tse-tung's thought has been the guide to the victory of the Chinese revolution. It has integrated the universal truth of Marxism-Leninism with the concrete practice of the Chinese revolution and creatively developed Marxism-Leninism, thus adding new weapons to the arsenal of Marxism-Leninism.

Ours is the epoch in which world capitalism and imperialism are heading for their doom and socialism and communism are marching to victory. Comrade Mao Tse-tung's theory of people's war is not only a product of the Chinese revolution, but has also the characteristics of our epoch. The new experience gained in the people's revolutionary struggles in various countries since World War II has provided continuous evidence that Mao Tse-tung's thought is a common asset of the revolutionary people of the whole world. This is the great international significance of the thought of Mao Tse-tung.

DEFEAT U.S. IMPERIALISM AND ITS LACKEYS BY PEOPLE'S WAR

Since World War II, U.S. imperialism has stepped into the shoes of German, Japanese and Italian fascism and has been trying to build a great American empire by dominating and enslaving the whole world. It is actively fostering Japanese and West German militarism as its chief accomplices in unleashing a world war. Like a vicious wolf, it is bullying and enslaving various peoples, plundering their wealth, encroaching upon their countries' sovereignty and interfering in their internal affairs. It is the most rabid aggressor in human history and the most ferocious common enemy of the people of the world. Every people or country

2. *The Victory of People's War*

in the world that wants revolution, independence and peace cannot but direct the spearhead of its struggle against U. S. imperialism.

Just as the Japanese imperialists' policy of subjugating China made it possible for the Chinese people to form the broadest possible united front against them, so the U. S. imperialists' policy of seeking world domination makes it possible for the people throughout the world to unite all the forces that can be united and form the broadest possible united front for a converging attack on U. S. imperialism.

At present, the main battlefield of the fierce struggle between the people of the world on the one side and U. S. imperialism and its lackeys on the other is the vast area of Asia, Africa and Latin America. In the world as a whole, this is the area where the people suffer worst from imperialist oppression and where imperialist rule is most vulnerable. Since World War II, revolutionary storms have been rising in this area, and today they have become the most important force directly pounding U. S. imperialism. The contradiction between the revolutionary peoples of Asia, Africa and Latin America and the imperialists headed by the United States is the principal contradiction in the contemporary world. The development of this contradiction is promoting the struggle of the people of the whole world against U. S. imperialism and its lackeys.

Since World War II, people's war has increasingly demonstrated its power in Asia, Africa and Latin America. The peoples of China, Korea, Viet Nam, Laos, Cuba, Indonesia, Algeria and other countries have waged people's wars against the imperialists and their lackeys and won great victories. The classes leading these people's wars may vary, and so may the breadth and depth of mass mobiliza-

2. *The Victory of People's War*

tion and the extent of victory, but the victories in these people's wars have very much weakened and pinned down the forces of imperialism, upset the U.S. imperialist plan to launch a world war, and become mighty factors defending world peace.

Today, the conditions are more favorable than ever before for the waging of people's wars by the revolutionary peoples of Asia, Africa and Latin America against U.S. imperialism and its lackeys.

Since World War II and the succeeding years of revolutionary upsurge, there has been a great rise in the level of political consciousness and the degree of organization of the people in all countries, and the resources available to them for mutual support and aid have greatly increased. The whole capitalist-imperialist system has become drastically weaker and is in the process of increasing convulsion and disintegration. After World War I, the imperialists lacked the power to destroy the new-born socialist Soviet state, but they were still able to suppress the people's revolutionary movements in some countries in the parts of the world under their own rule and so maintain a short period of comparative stability. Since World War II, however, not only have they been unable to stop a number of countries from taking the socialist road, but they are no longer capable of holding back the surging tide of the people's revolutionary movements in the areas under their own rule.

U.S. imperialism is stronger, but also more vulnerable, than any imperialism of the past. It sets itself against the people of the whole world, including the people of the United States. Its human, military, material and financial resources are far from sufficient for the realization of its ambition of dominating the whole world. U.S. imperialism has further weakened itself by occupying so many places in the world, overreaching itself, stretching its fingers out wide and dispersing its strength, with its rear so far away and its supply lines so long. As Comrade Mao Tse-tung has said, "Wherever it commits aggression, it puts a new noose around its neck. It is besieged ring upon ring by the people of the whole world."[22]

When committing aggression in a foreign country, U.S. imperialism can only employ part of its forces, which are sent to fight an unjust war far from their native land and therefore have a low morale, and so U.S. imperialism is beset with great difficulties. The people subjected to its aggression are having a trial of strength with U.S. imperialism neither in Washington nor New York, neither in Honolulu nor Florida, but are fighting for independence and freedom on their own soil. Once they are mobilized on a broad scale, they will have inexhaustible strength. Thus superiority will belong not to the United States but to the people subjected to its aggression. The latter, though apparently weak and small, are really more powerful than U.S. imperialism.

The struggles waged by the different peoples against U.S. imperialism reinforce each other and merge into a torrential world-wide tide of opposition to U.S. imperialism. The more successful the development of people's war in a given region, the larger the number of U.S. imperialist forces that can be pinned down and depleted there. When the U.S. aggressors are hard pressed in one place, they have no alternative but to loosen their grip on others. Therefore, the conditions become more favorable for the

[22] The Statement of Chairman Mao Tse-tung in Support of the People of the Congo (Leopoldville) Against U.S. Aggression, November 28, 1964.

2. *The Victory of People's War*

people elsewhere to wage struggles against U.S. imperialism and its lackeys.

Everything is divisible. And so is this colossus of U.S. imperialism. It can be split up and defeated. The peoples of Asia, Africa, Latin America and other regions can destroy it piece by piece, some striking at its head and others at its feet. That is why the greatest fear of U.S. imperialism is that people's wars will be launched in different parts of the world, and particularly in Asia, Africa and Latin America, and why it regards people's war as a mortal danger.

U.S. imperialism relies solely on its nuclear weapons to intimidate people. But these weapons cannot save U.S. imperialism from its doom. Nuclear weapons cannot be used lightly. U.S. imperialism has been condemned by the people of the whole world for its towering crime of dropping two atom bombs on Japan. If it uses nuclear weapons again, it will become isolated in the extreme. Moreover, the U.S. monopoly of nuclear weapons has long been broken; U.S. imperialism has these weapons, but others have them too. If it threatens other countries with nuclear weapons, U.S. imperialism will expose its own country to the same threat. For this reason, it will meet with strong opposition not only from the people elsewhere but also inevitably from the people in its own country. Even if U.S. imperialism brazenly uses nuclear weapons, it cannot conquer the people, who are indomitable.

However highly developed modern weapons and technical equipment may be and however complicated the methods of modern warfare, in the final analysis the outcome of a war will be decided by the sustained fighting of the ground forces, by the fighting at close quarters on

2. The Victory of People's War

battlefields, by the political consciousness of the men, by their courage and spirit of sacrifice. Here the weak points of U.S. imperialism will be completely laid bare, while the superiority of the revolutionary people will be brought into full play. The reactionary troops of U.S. imperialism cannot possibly be endowed with the courage and the spirit of sacrifice possessed by the revolutionary people. The spiritual atom bomb which the revolutionary people possess is a far more powerful and useful weapon than the physical atom bomb.

Viet Nam is the most convincing current example of a victim of aggression defeating U.S. imperialism by a people's war. The United States has made south Viet Nam a testing ground for the suppression of people's war. It has carried on this experiment for many years, and everybody can now see that the U.S. aggressors are unable to find a way of coping with people's war. On the other hand, the Vietnamese people have brought the power of people's war into full play in their struggle against the U.S. aggressors. The U.S. aggressors are in danger of being swamped in the people's war in Viet Nam. They are deeply worried that their defeat in Viet Nam will lead to a chain reaction. They are expanding the war in an attempt to save themselves from defeat. But the more they expand the war, the greater will be the chain reaction. The more they escalate the war, the heavier will be their fall and the more disastrous their defeat. The people in other parts of the world will see still more clearly that U.S. imperialism can be defeated, and that what the Vietnamese people can do, they can do too.

History has proved and will go on proving that people's war is the most effective weapon against U.S. imperialism and its lackeys. All revolutionary people will learn to wage people's war against U.S. imperialism and its lackeys. They will take up arms, learn to fight battles and become skilled in waging people's war, though they have not done so before. U.S. imperialism like a mad bull dashing from place to place, will finally be burned to ashes in the blazing fires of the people's wars it has provoked by its own actions.

THE KHRUSHCHOV REVISIONISTS ARE BETRAYERS OF PEOPLE'S WAR

The Khrushchov revisionists have come to the rescue of U.S. imperialism just when it is most panic-stricken and helpless in its efforts to cope with people's war. Working hand in glove with the U.S. imperialists, they are doing their utmost to spread all kinds of arguments against people's war and, wherever they can, they are scheming to undermine it by overt or covert means.

The fundamental reason why the Khrushchov revisionists are opposed to peoples' war is that they have no faith in the masses and are afraid of U.S. imperialism, of war and of revolution. Like all other opportunists, they are blind to the power of the masses and do not believe that the revolutionary people are capable of defeating imperialism. They submit to the nuclear blackmail of the U.S. imperialists and are afraid that, if the oppressed peoples and nations rise up to fight people's wars or the people of socialist countries repulse U.S. imperialist aggression, U.S. imperialism will become incensed, they themselves will become involved and their fond dream of Soviet-U.S. cooperation to dominate the world will be spoiled.

Ever since Lenin led the Great October Revolution to victory, the experience of innumerable revolutionary wars has borne out the truth that a revolutionary people who

2. The Victory of People's War

rise up with only their bare hands at the outset finally succeed in defeating the ruling classes who are armed to the teeth. The poorly armed have defeated the better armed. People's armed forces, beginning with only primitive swords, spears, rifles and hand-grenades, have in the end defeated the imperialist forces armed with modern aeroplanes, tanks, heavy artillery and atom bombs. Guerrilla forces have ultimately defeated regular armies. "Amateurs" who were never trained in any military schools have eventually defeated "professionals" graduated from military academies. And so on and so forth. Things stubbornly develop in a way that runs counter to the assertions of the revisionists, and facts are slapping them in the face.

The Khrushchov revisionists insist that a nation without nuclear weapons is incapable of defeating an enemy with nuclear weapons, whatever methods of fighting it may adopt. This is tantamount to saying that anyone without nuclear weapons is destined to come to grief, destined to be bullied and annihilated, and must either capitulate to the enemy when confronted with his nuclear weapons or come under the "protection" of some other nuclear power and submit to its beck and call. Isn't this the jungle law of survival par excellence? Isn't this helping the imperialists in their nuclear blackmail? Isn't this openly forbidding people to make revolution?

The Khrushchov revisionists assert that nuclear weapons and strategic rocket units are decisive while conventional forces are insignificant, and that a militia is just a heap of human flesh. For ridiculous reasons such as these, they oppose the mobilization of and reliance on the masses in the socialist countries to get prepared to use people's war against imperialist aggression. They have staked the whole future of their country on nuclear weapons and are

2. The Victory of People's War

engaged in a nuclear gamble with U.S. imperialism, with which they are trying to strike a political deal. Their theory of military strategy is the theory that nuclear weapons decide everything. Their line in army building is the bourgeois line which ignores the human factor and sees only the material factor and which regards technique as everything and politics as nothing.

The Khrushchov revisionists maintain that a single spark in any part of the globe may touch off a world nuclear conflagration and bring destruction to mankind. If this were true, our planet would have been destroyed time and time again. There have been wars of national liberation throughout the twenty years since World War II. But has any single one of them developed into a world war? Isn't it true that the U.S. imperialists' plans for a world war have been upset precisely thanks to the wars of national liberation in Asia, Africa and Latin America? By contrast, those who have done their utmost to stamp out the "sparks" of people's war have in fact encouraged U.S. imperialism in its aggressions and wars.

The Khrushchov revisionists claim that if their general line of "peaceful coexistence, peaceful transition and peaceful competition" is followed, the oppressed will be liberated and "a world without weapons, without armed forces and without wars" will come into being. But the inexorable fact is that imperialism and reaction headed by the United States are zealously priming their war machine and are daily engaged in sanguinary suppression of the revolutionary peoples and in the threat and use of armed force against independent countries. The kind of rubbish peddled by the Khrushchov revisionists has already taken a great toll of lives in a number of countries. Are these painful lessons, paid for in blood, still insufficient? The

2. The Victory of People's War

essence of the general line of the Khrushchov revisionists is nothing other than the demand that all the oppressed peoples and nations and all the countries which have won independence should lay down their arms and place themselves at the mercy of the U.S. imperialists and their lackeys who are armed to the teeth.

"While magistrates are allowed to burn down houses, the common people are forbidden even to light lamps." Such is the way of the imperialists and reactionaries. Subscribing to this imperialist philosophy, the Khrushchov revisionists shout at the Chinese people standing in the forefront of the fight for world peace: "You are bellicose!" Gentlemen, your abuse adds to our credit. It is this very "bellicosity" of ours that helps to prevent imperialism from unleashing a world war. The people are "bellicose" because they have to defend themselves and because the imperialists and reactionaries force them to be so. It is also the imperialists and reactionaries who have taught the people the arts of war. We are simply using revolutionary "bellicosity" to cope with counter-revolutionary bellicosity. How can it be argued that the imperialists and their lackeys may kill people everywhere, while the people must not strike back in self-defence or help one another? What kind of logic is this? The Khrushchov revisionists regard imperialists like Kennedy and Johnson as "sensible" and describe us together with all those who dare to carry out armed defence against imperialist aggression as "bellicose." This has revealed the Khrushchov revisionists in their true colors as the accomplices of imperialist gangsters.

We know that war brings destruction, sacrifice and suffering on the people. But the destruction, sacrifice and suffering will be much greater if no resistance is offered to imperialist armed aggression and the people become willing slaves. The sacrifice of a small number of people in revolutionary wars is repaid by security for whole nations, whole countries and even the whole of mankind; temporary suffering is repaid by lasting or even perpetual peace and happiness. War can temper the people and push history forward. In this sense, war is a great school.

When discussing World War I, Lenin said,

The war has brought hunger to the most civilized countries, to those most culturally developed. On the other hand, the war, as a tremendous historical process, has accelerated social development to an unheard-of degree.[23]

He added,

War has shaken up the masses, its untold horrors and suffering have awakened them. War has given history momentum and it is now flying with locomotive speed.[24]

If the arguments of the Khrushchov revisionists are to be believed, would not that make Lenin the worst of all "bellicose elements"?

In diametrical opposition to the Khrushchov revisionists, the Marxist-Leninists and revolutionary people never take a gloomy view of war. Our attitude towards imperialist wars of aggression has always been clear-cut. First, we are against them, and secondly, we are not afraid of them. We will destroy whoever attacks us. As for revolutionary wars waged by the oppressed nations and peoples, so far from opposing them, we invariably give them firm sup-

[23] V. I. Lenin, "For Bread and Peace," *Collected Works*, Eng. ed., Progress Publishers, Moscow, 1964, Vol. XXVI, p. 386.
[24] V. I. Lenin, "The Chief Task of Our Day," *Collected Works*, Eng. ed., Progress Publishers, Moscow, 1965, Vol. XXVII, p. 162.

2. *The Victory of People's War*

port and active aid. It has been so in the past, it remains so in the present and, when we grow in strength as time goes on, we will give them still more support and aid in the future. It is sheer day-dreaming for anyone to think that, since our revolution has been victorious, our national construction is forging ahead, our national wealth is increasing and our living conditions are improving, we too will lose our revolutionary fighting will, abandon the cause of world revolution and discard Marxism-Leninism and proletarian internationalism. Of course, every revolution in a country stems from the demands of its own people. Only when the people in a country are awakened, mobilized, organized and armed can they overthrow the reactionary rule of imperialism and its lackeys through struggle; their role cannot be replaced or taken over by any people from outside. In this sense, revolution cannot be imported. But this does not exclude mutual sympathy and support on the part of revolutionary peoples in their struggles against the imperialists and their lackeys. Our support and aid to other revolutionary peoples serves precisely to help their self-reliant struggle.

The propaganda of the Khrushchov revisionists against people's war and the publicity they give to defeatism and capitulationism tend to demoralize and spiritually disarm revolutionary people everywhere. These revisionists are doing what the U.S. imperialists are unable to do themselves and are rendering them great service. They have greatly encouraged U.S. imperialism in its war adventures. They have completely betrayed the Marxist-Leninist revolutionary theory of war and have become betrayers of people's war.

To win the struggle against U.S. imperialism and carry people's wars to victory, the Marxist-Leninists and revo-

257

2. The Victory of People's War

lutionary people throughout the world must resolutely oppose Khrushchov revisionism.

Today, Khrushchov revisionism has a dwindling audience among the revolutionary people of the world. Wherever there is armed aggression and suppression by imperialism and its lackeys, there are bound to be people's wars against aggression and oppression. It is certain that such wars will develop vigorously. This is an objective law independent of the will of either the U.S. imperialists or the Khrushchov revisionists. The revolutionary people of the world will sweep away everything that stands in the way of their advance. Khrushchov is finished. And the successors to Khrushchov revisionism will fare no better. The imperialists, the reactionaries and the Khrushchov revisionists, who have all set themselves against people's war, will be swept like dust from the stage of history by the mighty broom of the revolutionary people.

* * *

Great changes have taken place in China and the world in the twenty years since the victory of the War of Resistance Against Japan, changes that have made the situation more favorable than ever for the revolutionary people of the world and more unfavorable than ever for imperialism and its lackeys.

When Japanese imperialism launched its war of aggression against China, the Chinese people had only a very small people's army and a very small revolutionary base area, and they were up against the biggest military despot of the East. Yet even then, Comrade Mao Tse-tung said that the Chinese people's war could be won and that Japanese imperialism could be defeated. Today, the revolutionary base areas of the peoples of the world have grown to unprecedented proportions, their revolutionary move-

2. The Victory of People's War

ment is surging as never before, imperialism is weaker than ever, and U.S. imperialism, the chieftain of world imperialism, is suffering one defeat after another. We can say with even greater confidence that the people's wars can be won and U.S. imperialism can be defeated in all countries.

The peoples of the world now have the lessons of the October Revolution, the Anti-Fascist War, the Chinese people's War of Resistance and War of Liberation, the Korean people's War of Resistance to U.S. Aggression, the Vietnamese people's War of Liberation and their War of Resistance to U.S. Aggression, and the people's revolutionary armed struggles in many other countries. Provided each people studies these lessons well and creatively integrates them with the concrete practice of revolution in their own country, there is no doubt that the revolutionary peoples of the world will stage still more powerful and splendid dramas in the theater of people's war in their countries and that they will wipe off the earth once and for all the common enemy of all the peoples, U.S. imperialism, and its lackeys.

The struggle of the Vietnamese people against U.S. aggression and for national salvation is now the focus of the struggle of the people of the world against U.S. aggression. The determination of the Chinese people to support and aid the Vietnamese people in their struggle against U.S. aggression and for national salvation is unshakable. No matter what U.S. imperialism may do to expand its war adventure, the Chinese people will do everything in their power to support the Vietnamese people until every single one of the U.S. aggressors is driven out of Viet Nam.

The U.S. imperialists are now clamoring for another

2. The Victory of People's War

trial of strength with the Chinese people, for another large-scale ground war on the Asian mainland. If they insist on following in the footsteps of the Japanese fascists, well then, they may do so, if they please. The Chinese people definitely have ways of their own for coping with a U.S. imperialist war of aggression. Our methods are no secret. The most important one is still mobilization of the people, reliance on the people, making everyone a soldier and waging a people's war.

We want to tell the U.S. imperialists once again that the vast ocean of several hundred million Chinese people in arms will be more than enough to submerge your few million aggressor troops. If you dare to impose war on us, we shall gain freedom of action. It will then not be up to you to decide how the war will be fought. We shall fight in the ways most advantageous to us to destroy the enemy and wherever the enemy can be most easily destroyed. Since the Chinese people were able to destroy the Japanese aggressors twenty years ago, they are certainly still more capable of finishing off the U.S. aggressors today. The naval and air superiority you boast about cannot intimidate the Chinese people, and neither can the atom bomb you brandish at us. If you want to send troops, go ahead, the more the better. We will annihilate as many as you can send, and can even give you receipts. The Chinese people are a great, valiant people. We have the courage to shoulder the heavy burden of combating U.S. imperialism and to contribute our share in the struggle for final victory over this most ferocious enemy of the people of the world.

It must be pointed out in all seriousness that after the victory of the War of Resistance Taiwan was returned to China. The occupation of Taiwan by U.S. imperialism is

2. The Victory of People's War

absolutely unjustified. Taiwan Province is an inalienable part of Chinese territory. The U.S. imperialists must get out of Taiwan. The Chinese people are determined to liberate Taiwan.

In commemorating the 20th anniversary of victory in the War of Resistance Against Japan, we must also point out in all solemnity that the Japanese militarists fostered by U.S. imperialism will certainly receive still severer punishment if they ignore the firm opposition of the Japanese people and the people of Asia, again indulge in their pipedreams and resume their old road of aggression in Asia.

U.S. imperialism is preparing a world war. But can this save it from its doom? World War I was followed by the birth of the socialist Soviet Union. World War II was followed by the emergence of a series of socialist countries and many nationally independent countries. If the U.S. imperialists should insist on launching a third world war, it can be stated categorically that many more hundreds of millions of people will turn to socialism; the imperialists will then have little room left on the globe; and it is possible that the whole structure of imperialism will collapse.

We are optimistic about the future of the world. We are confident that the people will bring to an end the epoch of wars in human history. Comrade Mao Tse-tung pointed out long ago that war, this monster, "will be finally eliminated by the progress of human society, and in the not too distant future too. But there is only one way to eliminate it and that is to oppose war with war, to oppose counter-revolutionary war with revolutionary war."[25]

All peoples suffering from U.S. imperialist aggression, oppression and plunder, unite! Hold aloft the just banner

[25] Mao Tse-tung, "Problems of Strategy in China's Revolutionary War," *Selected Works*, Eng. ed., FLP, Peking, 1965, Vol. I, p. 182.

2. *The Victory of People's War*

of people's war and fight for the cause of world peace, national liberation, people's democracy and socialism! Victory will certainly go to the people of the world!

Long live the victory of people's war!

*Decision of
the Chinese Communist Party
Central Committee
Concerning the
Great Cultural Revolution*

(Adopted on August 8, 1966)

From the Survey of the China Mainland Press,
August 16, 1966 (No. 3761).

I. A NEW STAGE OF THE SOCIALIST REVOLUTION

The current great proletarian cultural revolution is a great revolution that touches people to their very souls, representing a more intensive and extensive new stage of the development of socialist revolution in our country.

At the 10th Plenary Session of the 8th Central Committee of the Party Comrade Mao Tse-tung said: In order to overthrow a political regime, it is always necessary to prepare the public opinion and carry out work in the ideological field in advance. This is true of the revolutionary class as well as of the counter-revolutionary class. Practice proves that this assertion of Comrade Mao Tse-tung is entirely correct.

3. The Great Cultural Revolution

Although the bourgeoisie have been overthrown, yet they attempt to use the old ideas, old culture, old customs, and old habits of the exploiting classes to corrupt the mind of man and conquer his heart in a bid to attain the goal of restoring their rule. On the other hand, the proletariat must squarely face all challenges of the bourgeoisie in the ideological sphere, and use its own new ideas, new culture, new customs and new habits to transform the spiritual aspect of the whole society.

At present, our aim is to knock down those power holders who take the capitalist road, criticize the bourgeois reactionary academic "authorities," criticize the ideologies of the bourgeoisie and all exploiting classes, reform education and literature and the arts, and reform all superstructure which is incompatible with the socialist economic base in order to facilitate the consolidation and development of the socialist system.

II. THE MAIN STREAM AND TWISTS AND TURNS

The broad masses of workers, peasants and soldiers, revolutionary intellectuals and revolutionary cadres constitute the main force in this great cultural revolution. Large numbers of revolutionary youngsters, hitherto unknown, have become brave vanguards. They have energy and wisdom. Using big-character posters and debates, they are airing their views and opinions in a big way, exposing and criticizing in a big way, firmly launching an attack against those open and covert bourgeois representatives. In such a great revolutionary movement, it is inevitable for them to have this or that shortcoming, but their revolutionary direction is right from beginning to end. This is the mainstream of the great proletarian cultural revolution. The revolution is continuing its march along this direction.

3. The Great Cultural Revolution

The cultural revolution, being a revolution, will unavoidably meet with resistance, which stems mainly from those power holders who have sneaked into the Party and who take the capitalist road. It also comes from the force of old social habits. Such resistance is still rather great and stubborn at present. But the great proletarian cultural revolution is a general trend of the time and cannot be resisted. A mass of facts show that if only the masses are fully aroused to action, such resistance will break down quickly.

Owing to the relative great resistance, the struggle may suffer one or several setbacks. Such setbacks will not cause any harm, however. They will only enable the proletarians and other sections of the laboring masses, especially the young ones, to temper themselves, to gain experience and learn lessons, to know that the road of revolution is tortuous and not smooth and straight.

III. THE WORD "COURAGE" MUST BE GIVEN FIRST PLACE AND THE MASSES MOBILIZED WITH A FREE HAND

Whether the leadership of the Party dares to mobilize the masses with a free hand will decide the fate of this great cultural revolution.

At the moment, Party organizations at various levels fall into four categories so far as their leadership of the cultural revolutionary movement is concerned.

(1) Some are able to stand in the van of the movement, daring to mobilize the masses with a free hand. Showing "courage," they are communist fighters who have nothing to fear and good pupils of Chairman Mao. By promoting big-character posters and large-scale debates, they encourage the masses to uncover all demons and monsters, while at the same time encouraging the masses to criticize the shortcomings and mistakes in their work. Such correct leader-

ship stems from the fact that proletarian politics is brought to the fore and the thought of Mao Tse-tung placed in the lead.

(2) Responsible officials of many units are still not very clear and not very earnest about their leadership of this great struggle. Providing it with weak leadership, they find themselves in a weak and impotent position. Showing "fear" at every turn, they stick to old rules and regulations, unwilling to break the conventions or seek progress. They are taken by surprise by the revolutionary new order of the masses, with the consequence that their leadership lags behind the situation and the masses.

(3) The responsible members of some units make this or that mistake in ordinary times. They are timid and afraid that the masses may pounce on their pigtails [mistakes]. In point of fact, so long as they earnestly conduct self-criticism and accept the criticisms of the masses, they will be forgiven by the Party and the masses. Unless they do so, they will continue to make mistakes, thus becoming stumbling blocks to the mass movement.

(4) Some units are controlled by power holders who have sneaked into the Party and who take the capitalist road. These power holders are extremely afraid that the masses may expose them, and so they find various excuses to suppress the mass movement. Using the tactic of diverting attention from the target and confusing black and white, they attempt to lead the movement astray. When they feel extremely isolated and think that they cannot keep on going their own way, they may execute further plots, shoot at people in the back, manufacture rumors, and do their best to confuse the boundary line between revolution and counter-revolution in order to attack the revolutionaries.

3. The Great Cultural Revolution

The Party Central Committee requires Party committees at various levels to uphold correct leadership, be courageous, mobilize the masses with a free hand, change their state of weakness and impotency, encourage those comrades who have made mistakes but who are willing to make amends to lay down their packs and join the battle, and dismiss the power holders who take the capitalist road, so as to let the leadership return to the hands of proletarian revolutionaries.

IV. LET THE MASSES EDUCATE THEMSELVES IN THE MOVEMENT

In the great proletarian cultural revolution, it is the masses who must liberate themselves. We cannot do the things for them which they should do themselves.

We must trust the masses, rely on them, and respect their creative spirit. We must get rid of the word "fear." We must not be afraid of trouble. Chairman Mao has always told us that revolution is not an elegant, gentle, kind and genial thing. In this great revolutionary movement the masses must be told to educate themselves, to discern what is right and what is wrong, and which ways of doing things are correct and which are incorrect.

Full use must be made of such means as big-character posters and large-scale debates so that views and opinions may be aired and the masses helped to elucidate the correct viewpoints, criticize the erroneous opinions, and uncover all demons and monsters. Only in this way will it be possible to make the broad masses heighten their consciousness in the midst of struggle, increase their capacity for work, and distinguish between the right and wrong and the enemies and ourselves.

3. *The Great Cultural Revolution*

Who is our enemy and who is our friend? This question is a primary question of the revolution, as well as a primary question of the cultural revolution.

The Party leadership must be good at discovering the leftists, developing and expanding the ranks of the leftists, and resolutely relying on the revolutionary leftists. Only in this way can we in the movement completely isolate the mass of reactionary rightists, win over the middle-of-the-roaders, and rally the great majority. Through the movement we shall then ultimately unite with over 95 percent of the cadres and with over 95 percent of the masses.

Forces should be concentrated on attacking a handful of extremely reactionary bourgeois rightists and counter-revolutionary revisionists. Their anti-Party, anti-socialist, and anti-thought-of-Mao Tse-tung crimes must be fully exposed and criticized, and they must be isolated to the maximum extent.

The focus of this movement is on the purge of those power holders within the Party who take the capitalist road.

A strict distinction must be drawn between the anti-Party and anti-socialist rightists and those who support the Party and socialism but who have made some wrong remarks, done some wrong things, or written some bad articles or books.

A strict distinction must also be drawn between the bourgeois reactionary scholar-tyrants and reactionary "authorities" and people who hold bourgeois academic ideas of a general nature.

3. The Great Cultural Revolution

VI. CONTRADICTIONS AMONG THE PEOPLE MUST BE CORRECTLY HANDLED

It is necessary to strictly separate the two kinds of contradictions of different character—those among the people and those between the enemy and ourselves. Contradictions among the people must not be treated as contradictions between the enemy and ourselves or the other way round.

That differing opinions are found among the people is a normal phenomenon. Controversy between various kinds of opinion is not only unavoidable but necessary and beneficial. In the course of normal and unreserved debates the masses are capable of affirming what is correct and rectifying what is wrong, and gradually attaining unanimity.

In the course of debate, it is essential to adopt the method of putting facts on the table, explaining the reasons, and convincing people with truth. To the minority of people who hold different opinions the method of suppression must not be applied. The minority must be protected because sometimes truth is in the hand of the minority. Even if the opinions of the minority were wrong, they should be permitted to put forward their arguments and to reserve their own opinions.

In the course of the debates, people may argue with one another but must not use their fists.

In the course of debate, every revolutionary must be good at independent thinking, promoting the communist spirit of daring to think, speak, and act. Under the premise of a direction, a revolutionary comrade should not argue endlessly on questions of technicalities in order to strengthen solidarity.

3. *The Great Cultural Revolution*

VII. BE ALERT AGAINST THOSE WHO LABEL REVOLUTIONARY MASSES AS "COUNTER-REVOLUTIONARIES"

In some schools, some units and some work teams, responsible members have organized a counter-attack against the masses who posted big-character wall newspapers against them. They even intimated that to oppose the leaders of their own units or work teams was to oppose the Party Central Committee, the Party and socialism, and that any slogan shouted in this regard was a counter-revolutionary slogan. By so doing they will necessarily attack some real revolutionary activists. This is a wrong direction to take and a wrong line to follow. It is impermissible to do so.

Some who are seriously affected by erroneous thinking, and even some anti-Party and anti-socialist rightists, make use of certain shortcomings and mistakes in the mass movement to spread rumors and carry out instigations, purposely representing some masses as "counter-revolutionaries." We must beware of such "pickpockets," and expose their tricks in time.

In the movement, with the exception of existing counter-revolutionaries who have been proved to have committed murders, arson, poison spreading, sabotage and stealing of State secrets and who should be dealt with in accordance with law, problems among students of universities, specialized colleges, middle schools and primary schools should not lead to their purge. In order to prevent the shifting of the main target of struggle, it is impermissible to use any excuse to instigate the masses to struggle against the masses and students to struggle against students. Even in the case of real rightists, they should be dealt with in the light of prevailing circumstances at a late period in the movement.

3. The Great Cultural Revolution

Cadres may generally be classified into four types:
(1) The good.
(2) The relatively good.
(3) Those with serious mistakes but who are not anti-Party and anti-socialist elements.
(4) A small number of anti-Party and anti-socialist rightists.

Under general conditions, the first two types of cadres (the good and the relatively good) are in the majority.

Anti-Party and anti-socialist rightists must be fully exposed and knocked down, their influence must be eliminated and at the same time they should be given a chance to start anew.

IX. CULTURAL REVOLUTIONARY GROUPS, CULTURAL REVOLUTIONARY COMMITTEES, AND CULTURAL REVOLUTIONARY CONGRESSES

In the course of the great proletarian cultural revolution, many new things have begun to appear. In many schools and units, such organizational forms as cultural revolutionary groups and cultural revolutionary committees created by the masses are new things of great historic significance.

Cultural revolutionary groups, cultural revolutionary committees and cultural revolutionary congresses are the best new organizational forms for the self-education of the masses under the leadership of the Communist Party. They are the best bridges for strengthening the contact between the Party and the masses. They are power organs of the proletarian cultural revolution.

The struggle of the proletariat against old ideas, old culture, old customs and old habits left over from all exploiting classes for the past thousands of years will take a very long time. In view of this, cultural revolutionary groups, cultural revolutionary committees, and cultural revolutionary congresses should not be temporary organizations but should be permanent mass organizations. They are applicable not only to schools and organs but basically also to industrial and mining enterprises, streets and the countryside.

Members of the cultural revolutionary groups and cultural revolutionary committees and delegates to the cultural revolutionary congresses must be fully elected as in the Paris Commune. The name list of the candidates must be drawn up and submitted by the revolutionary masses, and after repeated discussions by the masses elections may then be held.

Members of the cultural revolutionary groups and cultural revolutionary committees and delegates to the cultural revolutionary congresses may be criticized by the masses at any time and, if they are found to be derelict in their duties, may be replaced by election after discussion by the masses.

In schools, cultural revolutionary groups, cultural revolutionary committees and cultural revolutionary congresses should take revolutionary students as the mainstay. At the same time, a certain number of revolutionary teachers and staff members should participate in them.

X. TEACHING REFORM

Reforming the old educational system and the old policy and method of teaching is an extremely vital task of the great proletarian cultural revolution.

In this great cultural revolution, it is necessary to completely change the situation where our schools are dominated by bourgeois intellectuals.

3. The Great Cultural Revolution

In schools of all types, it is imperative to carry out the policy, advanced by Comrade Mao Tse-tung, of making education serve proletarian politics and having education integrated with productive labor, so that those who get an education may develop morally, intellectually and physically and become socialist-minded, cultured laborers.

The academic course must be shortened and the curricula simplified. Teaching materials must be thoroughly reformed, and the more complex material must be simplified first of all. Students should take as their main task the study of their proper courses and also learn other things. Besides studying academic subjects, they should also learn to do industrial, agricultural and military work. They must also be prepared to participate in the cultural revolutionary struggle for criticizing the bourgeoisie.

XI. THE QUESTION OF CRITICISM BY NAME IN THE PRESS

In carrying out the cultural revolutionary mass movement, it is essential to combine the dissemination of the proletarian world outlook, Marxism-Leninism and the thought of Mao Tse-tung with the criticism of the bourgeois and feudal ideologies.

It is necessary to organize criticism of those bourgeois representatives who have wormed their way into the Party and the bourgeois reactionary academic "authorities," including the criticism of various reactionary viewpoints on all fronts of philosophy, history, political economy, education, literature and art, literary and art theory, and theory of natural sciences.

Criticism by name in the press must first be discussed by the Party committees at the corresponding levels, and in some cases approved by the higher Party committees.

3. The Great Cultural Revolution

XII. POLICY TOWARD SCIENTISTS, TECHNICIANS, AND WORKING PERSONNEL IN GENERAL

Toward scientists, technicians and [scientific and technical] working personnel in general, provided that they love their country, work actively, are not against the Party and socialism, and do not secretly collaborate with any foreign power(s) the policy of unity-criticism-unity should continue to be adopted in this movement. Scientists and scientific and technical personnel who have made valuable contributions should be protected. They may be assisted in gradually transforming their world outlook and styles of work.

XIII. THE QUESTION OF ARRANGEMENTS FOR COMBINING [THE CULTURAL REVOLUTION] EDUCATION MOVEMENT IN TOWN AND COUNTRYSIDE

In big and medium cities cultural and educational units and Party and government leadership organs are the key points of the present proletarian cultural revolution.

The great cultural revolution has made the socialist education movement in town and countryside even richer in content and better. It is necessary to combine the two. Arrangements to this end may be worked out by various localities and departments in the light of actual conditions.

In the countryside and in urban enterprises where the socialist education movement is carried out, if the original arrangements are suitable and are properly carried out, they should not be disturbed, and work should continue in accordance with the original arrangements. However, questions raised by the present proletarian cultural revolution movement must in a suitable moment be handed over to the masses for discussion so that the proletarian ideology may be made to flourish and the bourgeois ideology destroyed.

In some places, with the proletarian cultural revolution as the center, the socialist education movement is led forward, and one's politics, thinking, relations with one's organization and economic circumstances are made clear. Such practices may be permitted where the Party committee considers them proper.

XIV. GRASP THE REVOLUTION AND PROMOTE PRODUCTION

The great proletarian cultural revolution is aimed at enabling man to revolutionize his thinking and consequently enabling work in all fields to be done with greater, faster, better and more economical results. Provided the masses are fully mobilized and satisfactory arrangements are made, it is possible to guarantee that the cultural revolution and production will not impede each other and that a high quality of work in all fields will be attained.

The great proletarian cultural revolution is a mighty motive force for developing our country's social productivity. It is wrong to set the great cultural revolution against the development of production.

XV. THE ARMY

The cultural revolutionary movement and the socialist education movement in the armed forces should be conducted in accordance with the directives of the Military Commission of the Party Central Committee and the General Political Department of the PLA.

XVI. THE THOUGHT OF MAO TSE-TUNG IS THE GUIDE FOR THE PROLETARIAN CULTURAL REVOLUTION

In the course of the great proletarian cultural revolution, it is necessary to hold high the great red banner of the

3. The Great Cultural Revolution

thought of Mao Tse-tung and to place proletarian politics in command. The movement for creatively studying and applying Chairman Mao's works must be launched among the broad masses of workers, peasants and soldiers, cadres and intellectuals. The thought of Mao Tse-tung must be regarded as a compass to the cultural revolution.

In this complicated cultural revolution, Party committees at various levels must all the more earnestly undertake creative study and application of Chairman Mao's works. Particular stress must be laid on repeated study of Chairman Mao's works concerning the cultural revolution and the method of Party leadership, such as "On New Democracy," "Talks at the Yenan Forum on Literature and Art," "On the Correct Handling of Contradictions Among the People," "Speech at the National Propaganda Conference of the Chinese Communist Party," "Certain Questions of the Method of Leadership," and "Methods of Work of Party Committees."

Party committees at various levels must abide by the successive directives of Chairman Mao, implement the mass line of coming from the masses and returning to the masses, and be pupils first and teachers later. They must make an effort to avoid one-sidedness and limitations. They must promote materialist dialectics and oppose metaphysics and scholasticism.

Under the leadership of the Party center headed by Comrade Mao Tse-tung, the great proletarian cultural revolution will surely win a grand victory.

DOCUMENT 4

*Communiqué of
the Eleventh Plenary Session
of the Eighth Central Committee
of the Communist Party of China*

(Adopted on August 12, 1966)

From the Survey of the China Mainland Press,
August 17, 1966 (No. 3762).

The 11th plenary session of the 8th Central Committee of the Communist Party of China was held in Peking from August 1 to 12, 1966.

The 11th plenary session was presided over by Comrade Mao Tse-tung. Members and alternate members of the Central Committee attended. Also present were comrades from the regional bureaus of the Central Committee and from the provincial, municipal and autonomous region Party committees; members of the cultural revolution group of the Central Committee; comrades from the relevant departments of the Central Committee and the Government; and representatives of revolutionary teachers and students from institutions of higher learning in Peking.

The 11th plenary session after discussion adopts the

4. The Eleventh Plenary Session

"decision of the Central Committee of the Chinese Party concerning the great proletarian cultural revolution."

The plenary session after discussion approves the important policy decisions and measures concerning domestic and international questions adopted by the political bureau of the Central Committee since the 10th plenary session of the 8th Central Committee in September 1962.

DOMESTIC

At the 10th plenary session of the 8th Central Committee, Comrade Mao Tse-tung made a correct analysis of the situation at that time and once again stressed the theory of contradictions, classes and class struggle in socialist society. This is the guide for the socialist revolution and socialist construction in our country. Under the leadership of the Chinese Communist Party headed by Comrade Mao Tse-tung and under the guidance of the Party's general line of going all out, aiming high and achieving greater, faster, better and more economical results in building socialism, the people of our country have in the past four years unfolded the three great revolutionary movements of class struggle, the struggle for production and scientific experimentation, and have won great victories. The people's communes have been further consolidated and developed. An invigorating revolutionary atmosphere prevails in the whole country and the situation is one of a new all-round leap forward emerging.

The national economy of our country is developing steadily and soundly. The policy of readjustment, consolidation, filling out and raising of standards advanced by the Party's Central Committee has already been successfully carried out. The third Five-Year Plan started this year. On the industrial front, not only have big increases been registered in the output and variety of products, but their quality has also greatly improved. On the agricultural front, there have been good harvests for four consecutive years. The market is thriving and prices are stable. The success of the three nuclear tests is a concentrated expression of the new level reached in the development of China's science, technology and industry.

During the past few years, an extensive socialist education movement has unfolded in the rural areas, the cities and the army. At present, a great proletarian cultural revolution unprecedented in history is mounting in our country. The mass movement in which workers, peasants, soldiers, revolutionary intellectuals and cadres creatively study and apply Comrade Mao Tse-tung's works has ushered in a new era of direct mastery and application of Marxism-Leninism by the laboring people.

The plenary session fully approves the May 20, 1963 "decision of the Central Committee of the Chinese Communist Party on some problems in current rural work (draft)." It fully approves the January 14, 1965 summary minutes of discussion at the National Working Conference called by the political bureau of the Central Committee of the Chinese Communist Party: "Some current problems raised in the socialist education movement in the rural areas," that is, the 23-article document. These two documents were drawn up under the personal leadership of Comrade Mao Tse-tung and have been the powerful ideological weapon for our people in carrying out the socialist revolution. We should continue to act in accordance with the two above-mentioned documents and, in combination with the great proletarian cultural revolution, carry through to the end in both rural and urban areas the "four clean-ups" movement, that is, the socialist education movement

4. The Eleventh Plenary Session

to clean up politics, ideology, organization and economy.

The plenary session fully approves the series of brilliant policies of decisive and fundamental importance put forward by Comrade Mao Tse-tung over the past four years. These policies consist mainly of the following:

On the question of applying the principle of democratic centralism and carrying forward and developing the revolutionary tradition of the mass line;

On the question of raising and training successors in the proletarian revolutionary cause;

On the call for industrial enterprises to learn from the Taching Oil Field, for agricultural units to learn from the Tachai Production Brigade, for the whole country to learn from the People's Liberation Army, and for strengthening political and ideological work;

On the strategic principle of preparedness against war, preparedness against natural calamities and everything for the people;

On the question of breaking down foreign conventions and following our own road of industrial development;

On the question of system and deployment in economic construction and national defense construction;

On the call for the whole Party to grasp military affairs and for everybody to be a soldier;

On the question of planning and arrangements for the gradual mechanization of agriculture; and

On the call for the People's Liberation Army and all factories, villages, schools, commercial departments, service trades and Party and Government organizations to become great schools of revolution.

The plenary session stresses that the series of directives by Comrade Mao Tse-tung concerning the great proletarian cultural revolution are the guide for action in the

4. The Eleventh Plenary Session

present cultural revolution of our country; they constitute an important development of Marxism-Leninism.

The plenary session holds that the key to the success of this great cultural revolution is to have faith in the masses, rely on them, boldly arouse them and respect their initiative. It is therefore imperative to persevere in the line of "from the masses and to the masses." Be pupils of the masses before becoming their teachers. Dare to make revolution and be good at making revolution. Don't be afraid of disorder. Oppose the taking of the bourgeois stand, the shielding of rightists, the attacking of the left and repression of the great proletarian cultural revolution. Oppose the creation of a lot of restrictions to tie the hands of the masses. Don't be overlords or stand above the masses, blindly ordering them about.

Give enthusiastic support to the revolutionary left, take care to strive to unite with all those who can be united and concentrate our forces to strike at the handful of anti-Party, anti-socialist bourgeois rightists.

The plenary session holds that the series of questions advanced by Comrade Mao Tse-tung over the past four years concerning socialist revolution and socialist construction have greatly accelerated the development and success of the socialist cause in our country. These questions are of most profound and far-reaching significance for consolidating the dictatorship of the proletariat and the socialist system in our country, for preventing revisionist usurpation of the Party and State leadership, for preventing the restoration of capitalism, for insuring that our country adheres to proletarian internationalism and actively supports the revolutionary struggles of the peoples of the world and for insuring our country's gradual transition to communism in the future.

4. The Eleventh Plenary Session

The 11th plenary session of the 8th Central Committee holds that the present situation as regards the struggle of Marxist-Leninists and revolutionary people throughout the world against imperialism, reaction and modern revisionism is excellent. We are now in a new era of world revolution. All political forces are undergoing a process of great upheaval, great division and great reorganization. The revolutionary movement of the people in all countries, and particularly in Asia, Africa and Latin America, is surging vigorously forward. Despite the inevitable zigzags and reversals in the development of the international situation, the general trend of imperialism heading for total collapse and socialism advancing to world-wide victory is unalterable. US imperialism and its lackeys in various countries cannot avert their doom by brutally suppressing and wildly attacking the masses of the revolutionary people, or by bribing and deceiving them, on the contrary, this only serves to give further impetus to the revolutionary awakening of all peoples. The activities of US imperialism and its stooges in various countries against the people and against revolution are giving impetus to the revolutionary activities of all peoples. US imperialism and its stooges in various countries appear to be powerful but are actually very weak. Taking the long view, they are all paper tigers.

The new leading group of the Communist Party of the Soviet Union has inherited Khrushchov's mantle and is practicing Khrushchov revisionism without Khrushchov. Their line is one of safeguarding imperialist and colonialist domination in the capitalist world and restoring capitalism in the socialist world. The leading group of the CPSU has betrayed Marxism-Leninism, betrayed the great Lenin, betrayed the road of the great October Revolution, betrayed proletarian internationalism, betrayed the revolutionary cause of the international proletariat and of the oppressed peoples and oppressed nations, and betrayed the interests of the great Soviet people and the people of the socialist countries. They revile the Communist Party of China as being "dogmatic," "sectarian" and "left adventurist." In fact, what they are attacking is Marxism-Leninism itself. They are uniting with US-led imperialism and the reactionaries of various countries and forming a new holy alliance against communism, the people, revolution and China. But this counter-revolutionary holy alliance is doomed to bankruptcy and is already in the process of disintegration.

The plenary session holds that our Party's comprehensive public criticisms of Khrushchov revisionism over the last few years have been entirely correct and necessary. The "proposal concerning the general line of the international communist movement" advanced by the Central Committee of the Communist Party of China on June 14, 1963 is a programmatic document. This document drawn up under the personal leadership of Comrade Mao Tse-tung and the nine comments by the editorial departments of the *People's Daily* and the *Red Flag* on the open letter of the Central Committee of the CPSU, the article "A Comment on the March Moscow Meeting," Comrade Lin Piao's "Long Live the Victory of People's War," etc., give scientific Marxist-Leninist analyses of a series of important questions concerning the world revolution of our time and are powerful ideological weapons against imperialism and modern revisionism.

The plenary session maintains that to oppose imperialism, it is imperative to oppose modern revisionism. There is no middle road whatsoever in the struggle between Marxism-Leninism and modern revisionism. A clear line of demarcation must be drawn in dealing with the modern revisionist groups with the leadership of the CPSU as the center, and it is imperative resolutely to expose their true features as scabs. It is impossible to have "united action" with them.

The plenary session points out that proletarian internationalism is the supreme principle guiding China's foreign policy. The session warmly supports the just struggle of the Asian, African and Latin American peoples against imperialism headed by the United States and its stooges and also supports the revolutionary struggles of the people of all countries.

The plenary session most strongly condemns US imperialism for its crime of widening its war of aggression against Vietnam. The session most warmly and most resolutely supports the "appeal to the people of the whole country" issued by Comrade Ho Chi Minh, president of the Democratic Republic of Vietnam, and firmly supports the Vietnamese people in fighting to the end until final victory is achieved in their war against US aggression and for national salvation. The plenary session fully agrees to all the measures already taken and all actions to be taken as decided upon by the Central Committee of the Party and the Government in consultation with the Vietnamese side concerning aid to Vietnam for resisting US aggression.

The plenary session severely denounces the Soviet revisionist leading group for its counter-revolutionary two-faced policy of sham support but real betrayal on the question of Vietnam's resistance to US aggression.

The plenary session holds that US imperialism is the most ferocious common enemy of the peoples of the whole world. In order to isolate US imperialism to the maximum and deal blows to it, the broadest possible international united front must be established against US imperialism and its lackeys. The Soviet revisionist leading group is pursuing a policy of Soviet-US collaboration for world domination and has been conducting splittist, disruptive and subversive activities within the international communist movement and the national liberation movement in the active service of US imperialism. They cannot of course be included in this united front.

We must unite with all the people in the world who are against imperialism and colonialism, and carry the struggle against US imperialism and its lackeys through to the end.

Together with all the revolutionary Marxist-Leninists of the world, we must carry the struggle against modern revisionism through to the end and push forward the revolutionary cause of the international proletariat and the people of the world.

HOLD HIGH THE GREAT RED BANNER OF MAO TSE-TUNG'S THOUGHT

The 11th plenary session of the 8th Central Committee emphasizes that the intensive study of Comrade Mao Tse-tung's works by the whole Party and the whole nation is an important event of historic significance. Comrade Mao Tse-tung is the greatest Marxist-Leninist of our era. Comrade Mao Tse-tung has inherited, defended and developed Marxism-Leninism with genius, creatively and in an all-round way, and has raised Marxism-Leninism to a new stage. Mao Tse-tung's thought is Marxism-Leninism of the era in which imperialism is heading for total collapse and socialism is advancing to world-wide victory. It is the guiding principle for all the work of our Party and country. The plenary session holds that Comrade Lin Piao's call on the People's Liberation Army to launch a mass movement in the army to study Comrade Mao Tse-tung's works has set a brilliant example for the whole Party and the whole nation. The most reliable and fundamental guarantee against revisionism and the restoration of capitalism and for victory of our socialist and communist cause is to arm the masses of workers, peasants, soldiers, revolutionary intellectuals and cadres with Mao Tse-tung's thought and to promote the revolutionizing of people's ideology. The method of studying Comrade Mao Tse-tung's works with problems in mind, studying and applying his works in a creative way, combining study with practice, studying first what is urgently needed so as to get quick results, and of making great efforts in applying what one studies has proved effective and universally suitable and should be further popularized throughout the Party and the country.

The Communist Party of China is a great, glorious and correct party. Founded and fostered by Comrade Mao Tse-tung, ours is a party armed with Marxism-Leninism, with Mao Tse-tung's thought. Our Party is a proletarian vanguard that integrates theory with practice, forges close links with the masses of the people and has the spirit of earnest self-criticism. It is a proletarian revolutionary party which has gone through the most fierce, the most arduous, the longest and the most complex struggles in history. Our people is a great people. Our country is a great country. Our army is a great army. We firmly believe that under the leadership of our great leader, Comrade Mao Tse-tung, and the Communist Party of China, the armymen and civilians of the whole country, relying on their own efforts and working vigorously, will surely be able to surmount all difficulties and obstacles and fulfill the mission given by history, and will surely not disappoint the expectations of the revolutionary people of the world.

4. The Eleventh Plenary Session

The 11th plenary session of the 8th Central Committee calls on all the workers, people's commune members, commanders and fighters of the People's Liberation Army, revolutionary cadres, revolutionary intellectuals, revolutionary teachers and students and scientific and technical personnel of the country to raise still higher the great red banner of Mao Tse-tung's thought, unite with all those who can be united, surmount the resistance coming from various directions, from the counter-revolutionary revisionists and the "left" and right opportunists, overcome difficulties, shortcomings and mistakes, cleanse the dark spots in the Party and society, carry the great proletarian cultural revolution to the end, carry the socialist revolution to the end, and strive to fulfill the third Five-Year Plan and build China into a powerful socialist country.

We must be fired with great, lofty proletarian aspirations and dare to break paths unexplored by people before and scale unclimbed heights. We must do a good job of building socialist China, which has a quarter of the world's population, and make it an impregnable state of the proletariat that will never change its color. We must liberate Taiwan. We must heighten our vigilance a hundredfold and guard against surprise attacks from US imperialism and its accomplices. Should they dare to impose war on us, the 700 million Chinese people under the leadership of Comrade Mao Tse-tung and the Communist Party of China will certainly break the backs of the aggressors and wipe them out resolutely, thoroughly, totally, and completely.